The Dark Side of the Nation

The Dark Side of the Nation

Essays on Multiculturalism, Nationalism and Gender

Himani Bannerji

CANADIAN SCHOLARS' PRESS INC.   TORONTO   2000

The Dark Side of the Nation:
Essays on Multiculturalism, Nationalism and Gender
Himani Bannerji

First published in 2000 by
Canadian Scholars' Press Inc.
180 Bloor Street West, Suite 1202
Toronto, Ontario
M5S 2V6

CSPI acknowledges the financial support of the Government of Canada through the Book Publishing Industry Development Programme for our publishing activities.

Canadian Cataloguing in Publication Data

Bannerji, Himani
    The dark side of the nation: essays on nationalism, multiculturalism and gender

Includes bibliographical references.
ISBN 1-55130-172-5

1. Multiculturalism – Canada. 2. Minority women – Canada. I. Title.

FC105.M8B36 2000   305.8'00971   C00-930017-1
F1035.A1B275 2000

Managing Editor: Ruth Bradley-St-Cyr
Marketing Manager: Susan Cuk
Production Editor and proofreading: Trish O'Reilly
Page layout: Brad Horning
Cover design: Jean Louie

01 02 03 04 05 06   6 5 4 3 2

Printed and bound in Canada by AGMV Marquis

Contents

Acknowledgements

*T*hese essays owe a great deal to two people in particular, who provided me with the time, financial support and the institutional conditions to write them. They are Professor Leslie Roman and Professor Patricia Vertinsky at the University of British Columbia, Faculty of Education, where I spent the autumn of 1996 working on various aspects of multiculturalism and antiracism. I gave various seminars and talks on issues discussed in these essays at the University of British Columbia, Simon Fraser University, the University of Northern British Columbia in Prince George, Windy Pine Colloquium, Trent University, the Robarts Centre for Canadian Studies of York University, and at annual conferences of the Associations for Canadian Studies in Germany and Belgium. Among many colleagues I would especially like to thank those who have offered stimulating responses and actively encouraged me. They are Crystal Verduyn, Barbara Saunders, Shahrzad Mojab, Judith Whitehead, Dorothy Smith, Ato Sekyi Otu and David MacNally. I would also like to thank Davina Bhandar, Robert Gill, Michael Ma and Cheran Rudramurthy, all graduate students at York University who are themselves engaged in different ways in researching topics to be found in this collection, and with whom I have the pleasure of active working relations. Finally, but gratefully and definitively, I must thank my companion at home and in politics, Michael Kuttner, who has offered me help in ways that are too many to count. It is not a cliché to say that without him I could neither research nor write these essays.

Some of these essays have appeared in the following publications:

"On the Dark Side of the Nation: Politics of Multiculturalism and the State of 'Canada'." *Journal of Canadian Studies* 31, no. 3. Reprinted in Christl Verduyn, ed. *Literary Pluralities*. Toronto: Broadview Press, 1998.

"Geography Lessons: On Being an Insider/Outsider to the Canadian Nation." In Linda Eyre and Leslie Roman, eds. *Dangerous Territories: Struggles for Equality and Difference in Education*. London: Routledge, 1997.

"A Question of Silence: Reflections on Violence Against Women in Communities of Colour." In E. Dua and A. Robertson, eds. *Scratching the Surface: Canadian Anti-Racist Feminist Thought*. Toronto: Women's Press, 1999.

Introduction

To articulate the past does not mean to recognize it "the way it really was" (Ranke). It means to seize hold of a memory as it flashes up at a moment of danger. Historical materialism wishes to retain that image which unexpectedly appears to man singled out by history at a moment of danger. The danger affects both the content of the tradition and its receivers. The same threat hangs over both: that of becoming the tool of the ruling classes.

Walter Benjamin: Theses on the Philosophy of History
Illuminations

*I*f I had been told during the 1960s or 1970s that we would exit this century amidst horrendous economic and political crisis and faced with a threat of fascism, I would not have believed it. But this is what seems to have happened, with anti-imperialist politics in disarray and national liberation movements substituted by various right wing nationalisms or capitalist state inspired multiculturalisms which speak in the name of culture, tradition and identity. A reactionary use of the past and history, which Walter Benjamin noted during the era of nazism and European fascism, is being attempted again. There is the same attempt to reify history and aestheticize politics in the language of authenticity and culture in which, as Benjamin says above, "both the content of the tradition and its receivers" have become "the tools of the ruling classes."

Inspired by this sense of political emergency, the essays in this collection were written in the last five years. They primarily touch on political matters pertaining to Canada, where I have lived for the last thirty years, and India, the country of my birth, with which I still have both personal and research relations. But what I have noted and reflected upon has relevance for other countries as well. These essays attempt to capture the dark moods of our times as well as to search for spaces where resistance politics can grow. In the process of doing so I have been moved by the influence of Walter Benjamin, by his insights into the use of culture, the language of authenticity and identity as deployed by the Nazis and the fascists. Thus Benjamin himself has become one of those flashes of memories that he speaks about, which come up to us in our own moment of historical danger. We will not claim to recover him or his times "as it really was" (Ranke) — which would be a reificatory gesture — but use this memory, its flash, to light up however briefly and tenuously these new national cultural imaginaries, or officially or elitistically organized multiculturalisms.

Following Benjamin in his "Theses on the Philosophy of History" or his essay, "The Work of Art in the Age of Mechanical Reproduction" (1969), we can make a distinction between a reactionary or a crypto- or fully fascistic use of culture, and its opposite. The representational politics which claims to give us history or tradition "as it really was," free of changes brought on by its own movement as history, free of a content changed by its context, needs to be contrasted to a liberatory or emancipatory use of culture as a basis for political identities and agencies. Hence the understanding of history as flashes of memory in moments of danger is to be opposed to its treatment as an authenticating, totalizing narrative. Benjamin's thoughts on history, which are sometimes expressed in a language of messianism, of redemption of time, are coherent with those of Marx, and often inspired by a marxist sense of history and politics. In essays such as *The Eighteenth Brumaire of Louis Bonaparte*, which speaks of history in terms of its reified and reactionary use and explores the use of history as a mask of politics, Marx (1978) examines similar themes. These political masks, used by petty bourgeois reactionary forces, are masks of legitimation.

Through this puppet theatre of Roman antiquarian grandeur the French ruling classes in Marx's study accomplish their tasks of fascism. Thus dead traditions, or traditions of the dead, weigh like nightmares on the brains of the living. We need to ask, then, under what circumstances can culture become the material for organizing a politics of reaction and repression? Should our answer signal to Marx's quiet use (1978) of the notion of "hidden struggles" of classes in *The Communist Manifesto*? Unnoticed *as* class struggle, is a hidden class struggle being conducted behind cultural-historical masks of "authentic" identities, with the help of which our present day ruling classes seek to win a lasting victory? And remembering Gramsci, should we say that a counter-hegemonic use can also be made of culture?

My stand is obviously not that the use of culture in politics is always already reactionary, prone to becoming an alibi for fascism. If that were true then we would not see formulations and practices of a politicized culture as advanced by Benjamin, Bertolt Brecht and Gramsci, or its emancipatory organizational use, as in liberation struggles, by poets as different as Nicholas Guillen of Cuba and Ernesto Cardenal of Nicaragua. This way of thinking about the use of culture in contradictory forms of politics provides the theoretical and political problematic for the essays in this volume. It is from this point of view that I consider the political practice of the state and the ruling classes and their ideologues in Canada and elsewhere. We can choose to create different kinds of cultural politics, and, thus, to become or not become "tools of the ruling classes."

My problematic and essays in this collection also expose the fact that what we have come to call globalization is both an economic and a cultural imperialism. Moreover, the politics of the Western and third world ruling classes create a strong nexus between imperialism and these seemingly oppositional nation states. Thus the newly invented cultural nationalisms, such as in Iran or Afghanistan, speaking in the name of religion and tradition, have rooted epistemological as well as political-economic relations with global capitalism. Their invented ethnicities mirror those employed by racist/colonial discourses of modern western nations as manifested in their media and their actual military offensives against Iraq or Kosovo. The cultural stereotypes and ethnicizations used by these modernizing or rescue missions, which are also to be found in official or elite multiculturalisms of the West, are continuous with those used by right wing nationalist politics and nation states of the third world.

It is interesting that the rhetoric and some state initiatives of multiculturalism in the West are accompanied by the gathering strength of right wing politics. In Canada, among other things, there is the rise and consolidation of the Reform Party, while in Europe extreme right wing parties which are avowed supporters of Nazis have gained major electoral victories, as in Austria and Switzerland. Germany and France are full of neo-nazi groups, while in England the police are implicated in systemic racism. And everywhere in the West "immigration," a euphemistic expression for racist labour and citizenship policies, has become a major election platform. Thus, even in countries which are chronically unable to produce adequate population growth through birth rates, conditions of labour importation from third world countries and its regulation are major issues. The media and some members of the Canadian intelligentsia speak in terms of the end of "Canadian culture," displaying signs of feeling threatened by these "others," who are portrayed as an invasive force. In the meantime, Western capital roves in a world without borders, with trade agreements such as GATT and NAFTA ensuring their legal predations, while labour from third world countries is both locked in their national spaces and locked out from Western countries, marked by a discourse of illegality and alienness.

This imperialism, a.k.a. globalization, has not only destroyed socialist projects everywhere, but is on the verge of unravelling liberal democracies, especially in the third world. The rewards and compensations are to come from genocidal ventures based on the myth of pure ethnicities, where the dominant community gets the spoils of wars and pogroms, or international bodies such as NATO intervene to put in place equally obnoxious forms of acquisition. These political, military and economic performances use the slogans of freedom, democracy and sometimes multiculturalism in the West, and culture, god and identity in the third world — a rhetoric which often slides into a self-proclaimed anti-colonialism.

Under such complex political circumstances, with Marx, Benjamin and Gramsci on our mind, we need to think through the different discursive articulations and uses of multiculturalism. It is from this point of view that I speak of official or elite multiculturalism and of culture of resistance, or what I might also call popular multiculturalism. This type of cultural politics, if it is not to slide off into a vagueness and christian charitableness of tolerance, as with Charles Taylor, must articulate itself through a politicized understanding of cultural representation. Antiracist and feminist class politics must be its articulating basis. It is this which would prevent this popular multiculturalism from falling prey to colonial, racist discourse or to those of ethnic nationalisms. Such a popular framing of culture would not engage in fetishized and essentialized traditions. It would speak to multiplicities of tradition and power relations between them, marking the internal power-inscribed differences within the space of the nation, as well as in multinationalities. We could leave behind the Weberian paradigm of tradition-modernity and a facile post-colonialism which threatens to become a form of culturalism.

Of this double-edged politics of multiculturalism my concentration in these essays is on the one from above — on the politics of historical and cultural reification which creates political agencies for a racist capitalist state and its civil society. Such agencies and subjectivities have to be read within the realities of colonial and Canadian history, with formational peculiarities of a country such as Canada in mind, where we watch the contortions of a white settler society and state aspiring to liberal democracy. The Canadian state, for example, has a lot of work to do. It not only has to mediate and express the usual inequalities of a class and patriarchal society, but also the ones created through colonialism and racism which inflect class and patriarchy. It has to maintain some notions of individual rights and citizenship, along with a historically racialized hierarchy of labour importation and regulation and what David Theo Goldberg (1993) has called "racist culture." These historical and formational peculiarities of the Canadian state, its various manifestations of social relations of inequality, are discussed in detail in "On the Dark Side of the Nation" and "Geography Lessons." They particularly attend to notions of Canadian national culture and "multicultures" of the nation's others.

To understand this multiculturalism from above, to see through its various cultural/political masks, we need to understand the role and location of ideology within the state apparatus and the organized polity. To do so I have turned to Louis Althusser's (1971) concept of the ideological apparatus of the state and its complementarity with the repressive apparatus of the state. If we consider this official or elite multiculturalism as an ideological state apparatus we can see it as a device for constructing and ascribing political subjectivities and agencies for those who are seen as legitimate and full citizens and others who are peripheral to this in many senses. There is in this process an element of racialized ethnicization, which whitens North Americans of European origins and blackens or darkens their "others" by the same stroke. This is integral to Canadian class and cultural formation and distribution of political entitlement. The old and established colonial/racist discourses of tradition and modernity, civilization and savagery, are the conceptual devices of the construction and ascription of these racialized ethnicities. It is through these "conceptual practices of power" (Smith, 1990) that South Asians living in Canada, for example, can be reified as hindu or muslim, in short as religious identities. The essay "The Question of Silence" speaks to this political process and its social consequences particularly for women.

We need to repeat that there is nothing natural or primordial about cultural identities — religious or otherwise — and their projection as political agencies. In this multiculturalism serves as a collection of cultural categories for ruling or administering, claiming their representational status as direct emananations of social ontologies. This allows multiculturalism to serve as an ideology, both in the sense of a body of content, claiming that "we" or "they" are this or that kind of cultural identities, as well as an epistemological device for occluding the organization of the social. We are encouraged to forget that people do not have a fixed political agency, and as subjects of complex and contradictory social relations can be summoned as subjects and agents in diverse ways. Thus political agencies are not objects found on the social ground as immutable facts of life. The same woman or a group of people may be appellated as a class, religious or sexual agent depending on the ideological/political ground of interpellation within which she/it is being hailed as an agent. This fact comes out in debates on working class consciousness and class struggle, in discussions on the making of history and in notions such as class-for-itself and class-in-itself. If political agents were found objects, such debates would be inconceivable. In fact political organization and contestations would not be necessary. Taking a critical, anti-reificatory stand on the questions of cultural identity and politics shows us the importance of social analysis, theorization and organization. It becomes apparent that we cannot rely on immutable and predictable social subjectivities and agencies.

This idea of the malleable nature of political subjectivity or agency can serve for us as a point of intervention in the context of multiculturalism from above, whether conducted by the state or the national elite, its organic intellectuals. We can see how the ideological state apparatus, relying on a hegemonic racist culture, can form an interpellating device which segments the nation's cultural and political space as well as its labour market into ethnic communities. This results in fractured cultural communities, each with its ethnicized agents hooked into the ruling apparatus of the state and the social organization of classes. Defined thus, third world or non-white peoples living in Canada become organized into competitive entities with respect to each other. They are perceived to have no commonality, except that they are seen as, or self-appellate as, being essentially religious, traditional or pre-modern, and thus civilizationally backward. This type of conceptualization of political and social subjectivity or agency allows for no cross-border affiliation or formation, as for example does the concept of class.

Having a concept of class helps us to see the network of social relations constituting an overall social organization which both implicates and cuts through racialization/ethnicization and gender. The elimination of the concepts of class, gender and racialization and the construction of multicultural communities from above is particularly felicitous for all ruling classes and the states which express their ideological and socio-economic interests. In the case of Western elites and their governments, for example in Canada, Germany or the United States, it would no doubt be far easier for the states to tolerate or recognize cultural nationalism or religious

fundamentalism than class based social movements among the
immigrants and the "foreigners." It is a safe bet to say that if the
U.S. government had to choose between a revival of the left wing
Black Panther Party and a growing power of the Nation of Islam as
the burden of its tolerance, it would undoubtedly choose the latter
and offer cultural sensitivity as an excuse. It is the culturalization
of antiracist and other oppositional politics in the last decade or so
that has largely made it possible for the government of the U.S. or
of Canada to maintain the appearance of a democracy. In the United
States, for instance, this has allowed the once overt terror of the
state to mutate into a low intensity warfare against African-
Americans, First Nations and Latin Americans.

Though multiculturalism from above as proposed by elite
intellectuals has become a common phenomenon, there are very
few nations like Canada, where it has been pronounced by the state
as a part of its administrative apparatus. Such a step displays the
moral leadership of the state and fulfils its legitimation function.
The essays in this volume respond to this official gesture in different
ways.

Canadian official multiculturalism has developed through the
1970s and '80s, and has become in the '90s a major part of Canadian
political discourse and electoral organization. The development of
this discourse in Canada rather than in the United States, which is
also a multi-ethnic country, may be due to the lack of an
assimilationist discourse so pervasive in the U.S. The melting pot
thesis has not been popular in Canada, where the notion of a social
and cultural mosaic has had a greater influence among liberal critics.
This mosaic approach has not been compensated with an integrative
politics of antiracism or of class struggle which is sensitive to the
racialization involved in Canadian class formation. The organized
labour movement in Canada has repeatedly displayed anti-
immigrant sentiments. For any inspiration for an antiracist
theorization and practice of class struggle Canadians have looked
to the United States or the Caribbean. As class politics or class based
antiracism have not been generally popular in Canada, the political
space has been left open to the notion of undifferentiated cultural
or ethnic communities. In other words, Canadian political society
has reasons for being so open to official multiculturalism, and we

also need to remind ourselves of the timing of its appearance as a governing discourse.

Pierre Eliot Trudeau's gift of an official policy of multiculturalism appeared in our midst in a period of a rapid influx of third world immigrants into Canada, as well as in a moment of growing intensity of the old English-French rivalry. Quebec displayed tendencies of armed separatist struggles during the late 1960s and the early '70s. In this context the proclamation of multiculturalism could be seen as a diffusing or a muting device for francophone national aspirations, as much as a way of coping with the non-European immigrants' arrival. It also sidelined the claims of Canada's aboriginal population, which had displayed a propensity toward armed struggles for land claims, as exemplified by the American Indian Movement (AIM). The reduction of these groups' demands into cultural demands was obviously helpful to the nationhood of Canada with its hegemonic anglo-Canadian national culture. A political discourse relying on a language of culture and ideological constructions of ethnicized and racialized communities quickly gained ground.

This officially formulated discourse of cultural permissiveness, which echoes the liberal sentiment of plurality or diversity, had or has the merit of deflecting critical attention from a constantly racializing Canadian political economy. The effect of this occlusion can be seen in the writings and attitudes of non-white and non-European immigrants themselves, such as Neil Bissoondath (1994), who, subscribing to the myth of assimilation, wrote hostile journalistic tracts against those immigrants who seemed to resist it. It is not an accident that Bissoondath, who confuses between antiracism and multiculturalism, should fall for a political discourse of assimilation which keeps the so-called immigrants in place through a constantly deferred promise. In the multicultural paradigm, where difference is admitted, structural and ideological reasons for difference give place to a talk of immutable differences of ethnic cultures. In both paradigms as the focus shifts from processes of exclusion and marginalization to ethnic identities and their lack of adaptiveness, it is forgotten that these officially multicultural ethnicities, so embraced or rejected, are themselves the constructs of colonial — orientalist and racist — discourses. It is not surprising that many Western countries, including Australia with its infamous *terra nullius* clause regarding its aboriginal people, looked to Canadian official multiculturalism for ways to manage a colonial history, an imperialist present, and a convoluted liberal democracy. Official multiculturalism represents its polity in cultural terms, setting apart the so-called immigrants of colour from francophones and the aboriginal peoples. This organization brings into clearer focus the primary national imaginary of "Canada," to echo Benedict Anderson. It rests on posing "Canadian culture" against "multicultures." An element of whiteness quietly enters into cultural definitions, marking the difference between a core cultural group and other groups who are represented as cultural fragments. The larger function of this multiculturalism not only takes care of legitimation of the Canadian state, but helps in managing an emerging crisis in legitimation produced by a complex political conjuncture evolving through the years after the second world war.

Essays such as "A Question of Silence" and "The Paradox of Diversity" speak to these above-mentioned issues and show how the concept of diversity is deployed to achieve this end. Issues pertaining to gender or patriarchy also receive a theoretical priority in them. They speak explicitly about violence against women in these multiculturally constructed ethnicized communities. It becomes clear through these and other essays in this collection that no critique of hegemonic relations can take place by taking for granted the concepts of "the community" and "the nation" or by accepting the notions of "diversity" and "plurality" at their face value. These concepts or categories are ideological-political formulations reliant upon an anti-oppositional understanding of social and economic relations which constitute a much larger national and international political economy and their manifestations in our daily lives. Adoption of this critical view that neither "the nation" nor "the community" are spontaneous associations of people will reveal the roles played by class, patriarchy and gender in constructing relations and ideologies for a society and a state meant for ruling and exploitation. Thus a nexus is visible between the racialized class patriarchy of the Canadian state and its creations, the multicultural ethnic communities who come from equally sexist and class societies. There is a convergence of forms of ruling and exploitation when "the community" meets the multicultural state.

The essays in this volume try to put into practice a method of reading multiculturalism from above from the standpoint of antiracist feminist marxism. The essays on Charles Taylor and the paradoxical nature of the notion of diversity speak most explicitly to this method. They take up multiculturalism as what Dorothy Smith (1990), following Marx, has called an ideological or a ruling category, treating it as a discursive and practical category for mediating and augmenting the ruling relations of the Canadian society and state. They also show how it functions as an epistemology of occlusion which displaces the actual living subjects, their histories, cultures and social relations, with ideological constructs of ethnicity. Their anti-ideological critique adopts Marx's method of historical materialism that Benjamin advocates and rejects a separation between historical and everyday life and experiences of people and their various forms of consciousness. Only then can we observe the emergence of a critical subject who is a political agent rather than an ideological one. This critical stance allows for the return of the social subject and social organization as theoretical counters in our own political thought and practice. It even calls for a stylistic innovation of our critique, such as the one used in "On the Dark Side of the Nation," where a collaged experiential account serves as the point of departure as well as the social object or material moment for a marxist form of deconstructive social analysis. This approach should make it apparent that what is called "my experience" could only arise at the relational and historical junctures that I outline through the rest of the essay.

In *The German Ideology* Marx and Engels (1973) teach us to relate ideational endeavours, or forms of consciousness, to social organization and social relations. In their study of ideology and its critique this connection is the core which establishes acts of consciousness as "sensuous, human activity, practice." (1973: 121) This way of conceptualizing the relationship of thought to experience is a valuable antidote to the ideological one, since it annexes even the ideological into the territory of the social. As I have said elsewhere (Bannerji, 1995), for an individual, her knowledge, in the immediate sense (which we call "experience"), is local and partial.

But, nonetheless, it is neither false nor fantastic if recognized as such. It is more than the raw data of physical reflexes and feelings. It is the originating point of knowledge, the door to our social subjectivity.

The reason for this discussion of the relationship between experience and epistemology for critical analysis is that both among institutional academics and so-called orthodox marxists such a use of experience has not often been considered as valid. Knowledge for revolutionary social change has often denied the value of social experience. Even feminists who are socialists or marxists have not given the centrality to the experiencing subject that she deserves, as distinct from her economic functions, and have often adopted a dualist theoretical position. The tendency has been to dismiss the notions of subjectivity and experience as outgrowths of bourgeois individualism or psychologism. It is mainly marxist liberationist politics and cultural theories, preoccupied with the problem of representation and its relationship with history, class and culture, that have validated connections between social experience and a critical epistemology.

In conclusion I would like to say that these essays are small sketches which are created for a more in depth project which I hope to undertake on nationalism and multiculturalism. As they stand now, no one is more aware of their incomplete nature than I. But it is my belief that they point us to a necessary form of social and political theorization that has often been missing in Canadian cultural studies.

REFERENCES

Althusser, Louis. *Lenin and Philosophy*. Trans. Ben Brewster. London: Verso, 1971.

Bannerji, Himani. "But Who Speaks for Us? Experience and Agency in Conventional Feminist Paradigms." *Thinking Through: Essays on Feminism, Marxism and Antiracism*, 55-98. Toronto: Women's Press, 1995.

Benjamin, Walter. *Illuminations*. Ed. Hannah Arendt, trans. Harry Zohn. New York: Schocken Books, 1969.

Bissoondath, Neil. *Selling Illusions: The Cult of Multiculturalism in Canada*. Toronto: Penguin, 1994.

Goldberg, David Theo. *Racist Culture: Philosophy and the Politics of Meaning*. Oxford: Blackwell, 1993.

Marx, Karl. *The Eighteenth Brumaire of Louis Bonaparte*. In *The Marx-Engels Reader*, ed. Robert Tucker. New York: Norton & Co., 1978.

Marx, Karl and Frederick Engels. *The German Ideology*. Ed. C. J. Arthur. New York: International Publishers, 1973.

———. *The Communist Manifesto*. In Robert Tucker, ed. *The Marx-Engels Reader*. New York: Norton & Co., 1978.

Smith, Dorothy, E. *The Conceptual Practices of Power: A Feminist Sociology of Knowledge*. Toronto: University of Toronto Press, 1990.

CHAPTER 1

The Paradox of Diversity:
The Construction of a Multicultural
Canada and "Women of Colour"

Multiculturalism has acquired a quality akin to spectacle. The metaphor that has displaced the melting pot is the salad. A salad consists of many ingredients, is colorful and beautiful, and it is to be consumed by someone. Who consumes multiculturalism is a question begging to be asked.

Angela Y. Davis (1996, p. 45)

INTRODUCTION: COMPARING
MULTICULTURALISMS

omen of colour, diversity, difference and multiculturalism — concepts and discourses explored in this essay — are now so familiar that we are startled when reminded about their relatively recent appearance on the stage of politics and theory. Current political theorization in the West happens very often about and through them, especially when we speak of representational subjectivities and identities and political agencies. My acquaintance with the use of multicultural discourse, which implicates concepts such as women of colour, diversity and difference, among others, is restricted to anglophone western countries. And even among these I am most familiar with Canada and the United States, and also somewhat with Britain, while Australia still remains a distant reality. This essay particularly explores and critiques the uses of multicultural discourse, especially as it rests on the notion of diversity, in Canada, where I have lived long enough to study its emergence, and experienced the effects of its deployment in politics and our everyday life. I hope that my concentration on Canada, which has its own particular history and polity, will still help to throw light on discourses and practices of multiculturalism in the U.S., Britain, and even Australia, especially as an ideology for governing, as a source for organizing communities on the basis of racialized ethnicities. This offers a source of internal social differentiation and legitimation for various mainstream and official practices which extend from education at home to foreign policy for bombing Iraq. As well, comparison is always a revealing activity for exploring politics everywhere. I should mention at the outset that, whereas the discourse of multiculturalism with its core concepts of diversity or difference have a general cross-border or transnational appeal, the related agentic expression "women of colour" is primarily North American. Its use is not common in British feminist vocabulary, for example, where "black women" or "black and Asian women" are terms of choice. Also, women with African or aboriginal backgrounds do not readily respond to this name, as they consider themselves to have highly substantive cultural histories and special claims to the politicized notions of blackness and aboriginality.

But before we explore Canada specifically, we should begin by noting that the discourse of multiculturalism as used in Canada and the U.S. needs to be differentiated in one major respect. Whereas multiculturalism is a state initiated enterprise in Canada, with a legal and a governing apparatus consisting of legislation and official policies with appropriate administrative bureaus, in the U.S. that is not the case. This is not surprising because the historical and political conjunctures in Canada, with regard to state formation and national identity and its post-1950s image of itself as a "mosaic" society (Porter, 1965), are coherent with such an ideological elaboration by the state. The United States, on the other hand, with its war of independence from Britain, has been known for its longstanding and strong nationalism, its assimilationist or melting pot political culture, with a general drive to Americanize the cultures within its national boundary while also actively seeking an international cultural hegemony. This imperative directing ethnic cultures inside and outside of the U.S. to succumb to American culture, together with the fact that construction of "race" more than (racialized) ethnicity has directed class formation in the U.S. from the eras of slavery and industrialization until recently, when ethnicity of the Hispanic or Asian population is much in view, give multiculturalism in the U.S. a much more complex and ambiguous character than in Canada. There one can speak of multiculturalism from above or from below, whereas in Canada the case is somewhat different, since it is state initiated.

My impressions regarding multiculturalism in the U.S. come from reading both critical and creative literature, from anthologies such as *Mapping Multiculturalism* (Gordon & Newfield, 1996), *Multiculturalism: A Critical Reader* (Goldberg, 1994) and *Revolutionary Multiculturalism: Pedagogies of Dissent in the New Millennium* (McLaren, 1997), to name some of the more important ones. These representative collections, along with others, point to an increasing use of a culturalist/ethnicist discourse (often racialized) by the U.S. corporate and governmental sectors, while also indicating the lack of state-sponsored and centralized legal forms of multiculturalism. The anthologies speak to a basic contradiction. They disclose how governing in the U.S. continues to use an assimilationist universalism deployed through a language of liberal pluralism and citizenship, while also proliferating and relying on a language of racialized ethnicity of social and cultural alienness. Both at the level of common sense and administration this double-edged politics and the discourse of the alien and the illegal are so active that they manage to reduce affirmative action from an attempt at social justice into a "race" advantage question. Both this tendency of homogenization and the exclusionary use of cultural difference by government and economy, with a not-so-latent racialization, have been questioned from the populist left or left liberal perspectives. Many of the essays in these anthologies also seek to evolve a politics of radical pluralism or of radical democracy. They sometimes stretch the conceptual boundaries of multiculturalism from below to speak of not just radical democratic or social democratic, but revolutionary changes.

For this last group the discourse of multiculturalism has meant an entry point into an oppositional, or at least an alternative, way of contesting the dominant culture and making participatory space for the nation's others. This other in the multicultural context referred less to African Americans, who are linked more directly with the issue of "race," than to Hispanic or Asian American and white radical democrats, though of late increasingly it turned to African Americans as well.

To go from these general observations to more specific ones which support my claims, we need only to look at Gordon and Newfield's introduction to *Mapping Multiculturalism*. Dating the arrival of multicultural discourse to the very early 1990s, they carefully weigh out its pros and cons. They point out the discourse's potential (under certain circumstances) for providing "a major framework for analyzing intergroup relations in the United States" (Gordon & Newfield, 1996, p. 1), and its ability to confront racism and connect to "race relations" which are in need of major changes. Seen thus, multiculturalism becomes the heir to the deceased civil rights movement, and helps to disclose what Omi and Winnant call "dispersed projects" of racism (Gordon & Newfield, 1996, p. 3). But the perceived downside to multiculturalism was that in the 1980s it "replaced the emphasis on race and racism with an emphasis on cultural diversity ... and allowed the aura of free play to suggest a creative power to racial groups that lacked political and economic power" (Gordon & Newfield, 1996, p. 3). What Gordon and Newfield do not mention, but imply, is that this "aura of free play," this culturalization of politics, hides the hard realities of profit and class making in the U.S., and also establishes the centrality of an American culture by simultaneously designating other cultures as both autonomous and subcultures. A scathing criticism of multiculturalism as a tool for corporate America, both in terms of its internal diversity management and international capitalism or globalization, features in the essays. One of the strongest of these is the piece by Angela Davis.

Angela Davis's attempt to link social and economic relations of a racialized U.S. (international) capitalism to a critique of multiculturalism is partially offset by those who seek to use it for the creation of a coalitional subject, especially in the feminine. Here the concept of cultural hybridity, construed as integral to multiculturalism, gives it a populist or a radical face, as for example, in Norma Alarcon's (1996) conjugated subjects. For Alarcon, and others such as Chela Sandoval or Michelle Wallace, multiculturalism with its possibilities for cultural hybridity becomes a freeing discourse for subject construction which goes beyond the masculinized rhetoric of cultural nationalism or the fixity of a national identity (Sandoval, 1991). For Michelle Wallace (1994), as for Hazel Carby (1998) in *Race Men*, this is a conscious politics signalling a paradigm of multiple determinations and incommensurability.[1] This is where notions such as "border" identity, a new public sphere and so on become central.[2] For Peter McLaren (1997, pp. 13-14) multiculturalism can be revolutionary by giving him "a sense of atopy, indeterminacy, liminalities, out of overlapping cultural identifications and social practices," while Anzaldúa (1990) speaks to a multicultural subject and the importance of "making face" and "making soul."

It is interesting to note the relative absence of enthusiasm for multiculturalism among those critics who hold a political economic perspective and see it as an ideology for local and global capitalism and cross-border domination by the U.S. economy. Gomez-Peña (1996, p. 66), speaking about Mexican immigrants to the U.S. rendered into "illegal aliens," illustrates how neo-liberalism "under the banner of diversity," and thus of multiculturalism, renders "service to capitalist accumulation." (McLaren, 1997, p. 8) Michael Parenti (1996), in the same critical vein characterizes the U.S. as fascist, and speaks to the use of a multicultural discourse to create identities which McLaren terms (1997, p. 8) as forms of "ideological trafficking between nationality and ethnicity," while Jon Cruz (1996) speaks of multiculturalism's role in negotiating between global capitalism and the fiscal crisis of the state. This radical political economy perspective emphasizing exploitation, dispossession and survival takes the issues of multiculturalism and diversity beyond questions of conscious identity such as culture and ideology, or of a paradigm of homogeneity and heterogeneity as used by D.T. Goldberg (1994), or of ethical imperatives with respect to the "other."

The use of the discourse of multiculturalism in Britain is, as in the U.S., a complicated and voluntary affair. Unlike Canada, the British state has not put forward definitive legislation on this basis. Modes of governance regarding "race" relations or adjudication of racism do not seem to be conducted through a discourse of multiculturalism. Nor has multiculturalism or diversity management yet become an active instrument for the U.K.'s corporate culture in regulating or handling class or labour-capital relations. There may be some symptoms of multiculturalism emerging in the state and economy for management or containment of racialized class relations and exploitation, but they are far from being prominent.

As regards speaking from below, British antiracism is not primarily culturalist. It appears to have its roots in direct political organization against the British state and the economy — particularly regarding importation of labour through immigration and refugee laws and policies, as well as in the tradition of British labour politics (Centre for Cultural Studies, 1982; Gilroy, 1987). The struggle in Britain, it seems, has been much more structural than cultural, some cultural issues around the Bangladeshi and Pakistani muslim immigrants and citizens notwithstanding. The centrality of the dominant English culture, with its colonial self-importance dating back from the days of the empire, has not yielded to any talk of adjustment under the pressure of "other" cultures, though the large presence of immigrants from South Asia and the Caribbean has made some difference in literary and everyday cultural life — in novels, cinema, music or food habits, for example. In an official sense the state of Britain and its political ideology do not respond to diversity by gestures of inclusivity, but rather continue the "Englishness" that the era of the empire has created. Stuart Hall, Erol Lawrence or Paul Gilroy have all spoken extensively to this phenomenon, stressing the racist practices and cultural commonsense of the English national imaginary in books such as *The Empire Strikes Back*, while the journal *Race and Class*, edited from London by A. Shivanandan, or his book *A Different Hunger* (1982), speak to the racist imperialist capitalism of Britain and its highly racialized class formation.

Speaking of political subjectivities and identities, antiracist politics in Britain has largely developed under the umbrella of black and class politics. The notion "black," disarticulated from a biologistic connotation, has codified an oppositional political stance, and this is what Julia Sudbury, for example in *Other Kinds of Dreams* (1998), speaks to as she develops her thesis on black womanist politics of coalition in Britain. She tells us that, avoiding the British government's divisive naming of local non-white population as "black" and "Asian," women of the third world in Britain — i.e. non-white women — have called themselves "black." The term "black," therefore, is not a correlate of being African in this usage.[3] But Sudbury also points out that there have been and are contestations around this term, and we see that recently there are some direct allusions to U.S. popular multiculturalism by black British intellectuals. In this connection they speak positively of multiculturalism regarding possible alliances and coalitions among women and men of different ethnic groups living in Britain.[4] A similar left liberal stance on the question of political identity and agency has emerged in the works of Stuart Hall, for example "New Ethnicities" in *'Race,' Culture and Difference* (Hall, 1992). Hall's antiracist multiculturalism has drawn attention to "a self-representation, a conscious and strategic doubling of oneself and each other, a way of affecting not only the content but also the relations and politics of representation." (1992, p. 270) Similarly, Kobena Mercer spoke of "Thatcherite tillering through the shoals of minority demands," (Gordon & Newfield, 1996, p. 5) in contrast to the U.S. in the 1980s, where multicultural discourse had arisen, suggesting "a breakdown in the management of ethnic pluralism." (p. 5) Likewise Paul Gilroy, in *Black Atlantic* (1993), has been careful to move away from what Cedric Robinson (1996), denying "specular imagining[s]" of black and white (p. 116), has called the manichaeism of black and white fixed identities. This emphasis on changing, opening and hybridized identities of black enlightenment thought, which in Gilroy's case also speaks to modernism among black intellectuals, has probably also been evolved to keep a distance from black cultural nationalism, such as that of Louis Farakhan, or even the growing Afrocentric perspective of black American intellectuals such as Molefi Asante.

Whatever these complex reasons for different positions on multiculturalism may be, it is evident that black British use of multiculturalism, which has been both anticolonial and cultural in terms of political identities and agencies, generally came out of an antiracist and anti-empire struggle mounted from a class perspective. We will be hard put to find in it much of a statist multiculturalism. Instead we may find what we have called multiculturalism from below or popular multiculturalism. It is through the door of the notions of hybridity, openness and fluidity of identities, rather than strong state or ethnic nationalism, that a multiculturalist approach has marked "black" politics in Britain.

This same situation is evident in non-white women's politics in Britain. It encompasses intergroup politics, for example between African, Caribbean, Indian and Bangladeshi women, as well as politics between them, the white women's movement and the state. Here too we have the dialectic of universalism or sameness and particularism or difference as in the U.S., and sometimes this is left as an insoluble contradiction. New black women's politics, more womanist than feminist, moved away from the earlier, mainly white, women's liberation movement, to one where there was sought, if not always realized, a cohesion of different women. But the politics of grassroots non-white women's activism which Julia Sudbury records and analyzes has a strong antiracist component, and also a greater attachment to prevalent politics and political culture of the third world countries from which the women come.

This seems to have created a few important responses speaking to problems and divisiveness among non-white women themselves. Amina Mama (Anthias et al., 1992) has seen this type of womanist black women's politics as a facade for identity/authenticity politics, while Pratibha Parmar (1990) and Floya Anthias (Anthias et al., 1992) have spoken to both the divisiveness and points of identity among women. Others have spoken to the resentment among Asian women, who seem to feel that in spite of politicization of the term "black," it has meant African leadership in antiracist women's struggles (T. Modood, 1990). On the other side, there has been also a resentment among Afrocentric women who question the move away from Africa as a point of departure for antiracist politics, and resent the extension of this term to include others (see Sudbury, 1998, pp. 129-131). A very different take on all of this has been put forward by those who, excited by the notion of a post-modern, hybrid (feminine) subject of multiple and shifting subject positions, have approached questions of political subjectivity and agency from a radical multicultural position, similar to those in the United States. I shall mention two anthologies and a book in this respect, which try to go away from the language of blackness/whiteness: Floya Anthias, N. Yuval-Davis and H. Cain, *Racialized Boundaries*, K. Bhabnani and A. Phoenix (eds.) (1994), *Shifting Identities, Shifting Racisms*, and A. Brah (1996), *Cartographies of Diaspora: Contesting Identities*.

This discussion on the variations of the themes of multiculturalism and women of colour should make it evident to what extent they are dependent on context and location in terms of whether they serve the status quo or the opposition. Particularly in the United States, feminists have variously named themselves as women of colour, black women or third world women — often interchangeably — and wrote and organized towards the forging of a social politics in connection with coalition building towards social democracy, radical democracy and a multiculturalist, anti-imperialist feminism. I would like to draw attention especially to women of colour politics with regard to fashioning selves, social subjectivities and agencies, all of which touch the boundaries of identity. The two influential anthologies edited by Chandra Mohanty, Ann Russo and Lourdes Torres (1991) and Jacquie Alexander and Mohanty (1997) give us powerful versions of a radical, or even revolutionary, use of this term. Not unlike Britain, where feminist organizing has sought to create a space "by offering a form of affiliation that has shifted from sameness and commonality [with white or generic women] to the recognition of distinct social histories," (Sudbury, 1998, p. 11) non-white U.S. feminists have also used the notion of women of colour interchangeably with that of black women. Angela Davis, in her preface to Sudbury's book, does so quite unselfconsciously, indicating a routine practice.

Such unselfconsciousness is possible because of the radicalization of this term, women of colour, by anthologies such as *Third World Women and the Politics of Feminism*. The introduction of this book directly signals the radical political use of this term by equating women of colour with third world women as a mode for creating a "viable oppositional alliance."(Mohanty et al, 1991, p. 7) The authors claim that this "is a common context of struggle rather than color and racial identification."(p. 7) This "common context" is the same as "relations of inequality" which mark the entry of women of colour into the U.S. labour force, for example (p. 24). Mohanty, in her essay "Under Western Eyes," also makes it clear that "woman" is not a found meaning, but is a social subject and agent, a constructed category, and this construction takes place "in a variety of political contexts."(p. 65) This same oppositional antiracist position is clarified in Ann Russo's "Race, Identity and Feminist Struggles: We Cannot Live without Our Lives."(Mohanty et al., 1991) She too does not problematize the category women of colour, but contexts it to antiracist feminist organizing. As she puts it: "Simply adding women of colour to a list of women's issues, I would agree, actually leads to guilt and condescension, as well as to a partial and limiting politics and vision."(p. 301) The result of such add-ons is not an oppositional antiracist subjectivity for women of colour, but one of being constructed as "problems," "victims" and "special cases."(p. 301)

The same oppositional use is further developed in *Feminist Genealogies, Colonial Legacies, Democratic Futures*. Here the woman subject-agent is again called woman of colour or third world woman, with "aim(s) to provide a comparative, relational and historically based conception of feminism, one that differs markedly from the liberal pluralist understanding of feminism ...."(Alexander & Mohanty, 1997, p. xvi) This political-theoretical position which redeems the term woman of colour from liberal pluralism is expressed by Paula M. L. Moya in explicating and building on Cherrie Moraga's stance in *This Bridge Called My Back* (Anzaldúa & Moraga, 1983). Moya (with Moraga) rids the notion of its cultural pluralism by associating it with non-white, third world women's "flesh and blood experiences" in the U.S., and by extension other western capitalist democracies (Alexander & Mohanty, 1997, p. 23). She quotes Moraga about this "theory in the flesh" which "emphasizes the materiality of the body by conceptualizing 'flesh' as the site on or with which the woman of color experiences the painful material effects of living in a particular social location."(p. 23) Thus Moya builds out of Moraga a realist theory of identity, distinct from identity as projected by cultural nationalism, under the name of women of colour. Moya bares the nature of political identity advocated by Alexander and Mohanty and the opposition against which it is advanced. It needs to be quoted at some length to show her and their take on identity as both a socially grounded and a multifaceted affair:

> The problem posed by postmodernism is particularly acute for U.S. feminist scholars and activists of color, for whom "experience" and "identity" continue to be primary organizing principles around which they theorize and mobilize. Even women of color who readily acknowledge the nonessentialist nature of their political or theoretical commitments persist in referring to themselves as, for instance, "Chicana" or "Black" feminists .... For example, Moraga acknowledges that women of color are not "a 'natural' affinity group" even as she works to build a movement around and for people who identify as women of color. She can do this, without contradiction, because her understanding of the identity "women of color" reconceptualizes the notion of "identity" itself. Unlike postmodernist feminists who understand the concept of "identity" as inherently and perniciously "foundational", Moraga understands "identity" as relational and grounded in the historically produced social facts which constitute social locations.(p. 127)

This radical/oppositional take on the issue of identity obviously stems from what I have earlier called multiculturalism from below. It speaks to the forging of an oppositional/coalitional identity, to becoming rather than being born as a woman of colour as a process of an anti-imperialist political conscientization takes place among feminists. Alexander and Mohanty and the writers of the *Genealogies* anthology are explicitly critical of any subscription to racist-imperialist social relations and forms of consciousness, especially by feminists who claim to engage in counter-hegemonic politics.

This discussion of women of colour is incomplete without a reference to Patricia Hill Collins, who in her two books *Black Feminist Thought* (1990) and *Fighting Words: Black Women and the Search for Justice* (1998), has tried to create an epistemology of resistance, while also speaking of black or Afrocentric identities. Since the second book is a further development of the first, we will look at both her epistemological and agency theorizing projects. Her theorization of black feminist thought is one of specialized knowledge created in rejection of and opposition to the claim to universality of standard European academic knowledge. This universality actually turns out to be nothing other than the "interests of their creators" (Collins 1990, p. 15). The issue of social ontology or who produces any thought, then, is material for Collins, and she says: "At the core of Black feminist thought lie theories created by African-American women which clarify a Black women's standpoint — in essence an interpretation of Black women's experiences and ideas by those who participate in them" (p. 15). This position vindicates non-academic knowledge as experts' knowledge, thus reclaiming black women's intellectual tradition, generated from their everyday ideas. In this way black women — "mothers, teachers, church members and cultural creators" — become intellectuals (p. 15). Not just written sources but spoken word, oral traditions, and interactions of the community produce knowledge, and this knowledge, infused with "Afrocentric feminist sensibility" becomes the heart and body of black feminist thought (p. 16). At this point we might ask the questions about identity and political agency that Collins brings to us. It seems to be different from a coalitional approach in the use of women of colour or third world women (Alexander & Mohanty, 1997; Mohanty, et al., 1990), especially as Afro-American social ontologies or experiences are sources for black feminist thought. As Collins says, not anyone can produce black feminist thought. Can women from non-African descents be producers of black feminist thought? Interestingly Collins comes up with an inclusive and positive answer. She tries to disarticulate this notion from biology or even possibly from African history in the United States. "Separation of biology from ideology," she says, "must be made" (p. 20). You don't have to be African American to be a black feminist and produce that type of knowledge. By nature, Collins says, black feminist thought is deconstructive. Its task is "exposing a concept as ideological and culturally constructed rather than as natural or a simple rejection of reality" (p. 14). In this she signals to Linda Alcoff's position of 1988; her example of deconstructive knowledge is Sojourner Truth's problematization of the category "woman" in her "Ain't I a woman" speech. Collins continues her work of resistance epistemology in *Fighting Words*, and in this book explicitly speaks to black feminist thought's contribution to critical social theory (1998, p. xviii). In this text, written particularly to create an ethical-political agency for activists looking for social rather than sectarian justice, Collins does not resort to the category women of colour. To a large extent her radicalization of the term "black women" signals to the strand of British antiracist activism written about by Sudbury. Though still interested in Afro-centrism, Collins seeks to void that notion of its cultural nationalist and particularist context, thus leaving us with an interesting text full of tensions between a general ethical politics and a strong emphasis on the African diaspora's history of domination and resistance.

One could go on much longer on antiracist, anti-imperialist feminism in the U.S. One could also speak at length of the slide of multiculturalist discourse, with its core terms of diversity, difference and women of colour, into liberal culturalism, into its co-optation as a tool for what Angela Davis (1996, p. 41) calls "diversity management," that salad bowl corporate view of difference. But I will stop here, using this introduction as a broadly sketched background for my more limited project, consisting of an exploration of the term "women of colour" as a part of a constellation of ideological agentic and identity terms constituting multiculturalism in the Canadian context. The most salient aspect of this context is that multiculturalism is a state sanctioned, state organized ideological affair in Canada. Not just in Orwell's ideologically constructed communist dystopia, but in actual mundane granting/funding, in electoral policies and outcomes, in ethnic cultural fairs and religious celebrations, in court legal defences, this particular variant of multiculturalism organizes the socio-cultural, legal-economic space of Canada. This paper attempts to critically examine the particular meaning such a conjuncture provides to the notion of women of colour and its home space of the discourse of diversity and multiculturalism. In this, radical potentials spoken of above are substantially diminished.

CANADA: CONSTRUCTING 'THE WOMAN OF COLOUR' THROUGH MULTICULTURALISM AND DIVERSITY

People who are not familiar with North American political and cultural, especially feminist, language are both puzzled and repelled by the expression "woman of colour." I know this because this expression has become a part of my ordinary vocabulary in recent years, and often when I have used it in India my interlocutors, even feminist ones, looked puzzled or annoyed. Most remarked on what a strange expression that was, and others reminded me that I had reverted to a racist, segregational language of apartheid and the American South — a "coloured woman." Even when I tried to insist on the difference between these two expressions, these women were reluctant to relinquish this association. Their reaction reminded me of a time, my early years in Canada during the early seventies, when I learned and evolved my antiracist feminist politics without this word anywhere in sight. At some point it travelled to us from below the 49th parallel, and found a congenial home on our tongue.

The Indian women's response was similar to my own long years of reluctance to use this notion for any purpose of social analysis and critique. I speak of this in my introduction to the anthology *Returning the Gaze* (1993, pp. ix-xv) and in my essays in *Thinking Through* (1995). There I use the notion "non-white" for the purpose of creating an antiracist critique, maintaining that in the context of analyzing racialized social organization and relations, what needs to be stressed is the non-whiteness of this woman social subject of oppression. After all, it is on this basis that she is being oppressed or discriminated against, and others (white women) comparatively privileged. Every other particularity about this subject is built on this binary conceptualization and politics. But having said this, I have to admit that of late the expression woman of colour has crept up on me, especially when I am speaking in common language in my daily interchange with other non-white women who are doing antiracist work. They use it, as do their U.S. counterparts, as a term of alterity, or even of opposition to the status quo in spite of the statist nature of this concept in Canada, and so do I. The question is, how or why did this happen? What necessities or circumstances drew me into this orbit?

To answer this question I have to move back in time. I remember that one of the earliest occasions when I heard this expression was when I was invited to read poetry in a cultural festival. It was called something like Rainbow Women: Multicultural Women in Concert. It was organized by Faith Nolan, now a well-known black Canadian singer. I was struck by the notion of rainbow women, which, I was told, had to do with my being a woman of colour and bringing this colour to join others in a rainbow combination. I was not taken by this exercise. I found woman of colour to be both a coy and an offensive notion and, like many others, thought of the expression "coloured." I did not want to call myself this. Nor did I feel convinced of the capacity for resistance attributed to this notion, which encoded a multicultural unity, cherishing diversity, through promulgating a generic or homogenizing term which would cover all non-white others, mostly those who were not black. So there I had it, two groups of non-white women — black and of colour — arranged in a gradually paling hierarchy, with one end of the spectrum touching the darkest shade of colour. This colour hierarchy struck me then, as it does now, as an offensive way of creating social subjects and political agents. It falls back, even if unconsciously, on the hegemonic common sense of social culture and politics of slavery and apartheid. What colour are you, it asks: are you black, white, yellow, or brown? Shades of negative differences, of being considered mulatto, quadroons, octoroons (ideologies and social relations of plantation societies) lie behind this formulation. They are presumably promulgated in good faith, to fight racist-sexism and white privilege. It is also significant that most of the time this term does not refer to black women, or those of the First Nations. I was quite determined not to use it, but as the '80s rolled by woman of colour was Canadianized. She had, as they say in Canada about immigrants, "landed." And here I am using it every once in a while, for the purpose of intelligibility, to keep in step with my fellow antiracist feminists!

So what discursive revolution, paradigm shift, occurred in Canada during the '80s and the '90s which could have been hospitable to, or indeed embraced, this woman of colour? In my view, there are two broad political areas which need to be problematized. One could be called, following Louis Althusser (1971), the ideological apparatuses of the state, including its political and civil administration; and the other, the civil society (Gramsci, 1971), the everyday world of common social relations, values and practices of culture and power. We may begin first by speaking of the state, not because it was the first to name us as political agents in terms of being women of colour. It did not, as the term had a U.S. origin. But it provided the political culture for accepting, using and naturalizing a colour-based notion of subjectivity and agency, which in continuity with Canada's colonial formation came to dominate the cultural politics of Canada's other women. Canadians have been living in an historical and current environment of political colour coding, even, or mainly, when forging a liberal democratic politics for the country as a whole.

My claim may be more clear if I were to draw attention to the entry of official multiculturalism onto the Canadian political stage. The open door policy of immigration, especially attributed to the Liberal party and its charismatic leader, Pierre Trudeau, throughout the 1960s and '70s, had brought many people of colour, other "races," into the country.[5] The reason for this was the expectation of capitalist industrial growth in Canada and the aspiration to the creation of a liberal democratic nationhood. The former British colonies in particular provided cheap labour, both skilled and un-skilled, as well as the democratic grounds for converging otherness. Thus colour, the cognate of race, refracted into indirect notions of multi-culture and ethnicity, was much on the mind of the Canadian state, just as much as in the nineteenth or early twentieth centuries.[6] Unlike the radical alternative political-cultural activists, the Canadian state was careful not to directly use the notion of colour in the way it designated the newcomers. But colour was translated into the language of visibility. The new Canadian social and political subject was appellated "visible minority," stressing both the features of being non-white and therefore visible in a way whites are not, and of being politically minor players. It is at this time, at the urging of the National Directorate of Women and the Secretary of State, that non-white women made a niche for themselves in the mainstream politics by creating a representational organization, the National Coalition of Visible Minority Women.[7] This status of visible minority was not felt by a large number of women to be problematic or compromising, since they shared political values with the mainstream. Minor as their part was, set apart by their visibility, which was also the only ground of their political eligibility, they were content. Until then they were covered under the umbrella of immigrant women, a category that included and expanded beyond non-white women, who were also called third world women. All these expressions have remained in our political-cultural language, but visible minority women has become the strongest. A categorical child of the state, cradled by the Ministry of Multiculturalism and the Secretary of State, this expression underpins and is the mainstream counterpart of the more grassroots notion of the woman of colour. This popular feminist term actually relied for its political meaning and vitality upon the mainstream analogue and the same discourse of multiculturalism pertaining to visible minority women embedded in both state and society for its existential environment. With no interest in class politics, and no real analysis of or resistance to racialization or ethnicization, chiefly preoccupied with bureaucratic representation or inclusion for a very limited power sharing within the status quo, these political terminologies became current usages. The multi-ethnic, multinational state, with its history of racialized class formation and political ideology, discovering multiculturalism as a way of both hiding and enshrining power relations, provided a naturalized political language even to the others of the Canadian society. Not surprisingly, these expressions found their way into general feminist academic and activist discourse and into NGOs for women and into the political discourse of International Women's Day. In particular, visible minority women translated well into women of colour and that became the name chosen by alternative politics of Canada. This practice followed the United States, and it solved the problem of finding a name for building coalition among all women. It vaguely and pleasantly gestured to race as colour and, of course, to gender/patriarchy by evoking woman. But the concept of race lost its hard edges of criticality, class disappeared entirely, and colour gave a feeling of brightness, brilliance or vividness, of a celebration of a difference which was disconnected from social relations of power, but instead perceived as diversity, as existing socio-cultural ontologies or facts.

The suitability of woman of colour for Canadian political culture was such that no one did then, or does now, speak about the absurdity of calling white women colourless or invisible. As for the degeneration of powered difference into diversity, class analysis was, after all, not the main interest of the North American women's movement, while race was accepted by most as an existential, cultural fact, if not always a biological one. This political stance has led to the seeking for better race relations, in which feminists aspiring to diversity have participated. So the term unproblematically combined within itself both the common sense of race and the antidote of liberal pluralism. The apartheid notion of coloured woman stood behind and cast a long shadow over her modern sister, since it was the subliminal principle of intelligibility of this recent coinage, no matter how radically aimed.

Common sense of skin and colour, particularly in the colonial context, is old. Bodies — skin, facial features, height, build, and so forth — had been morally and politically signified for centuries in North America and Europe (see Gillman, 1985). Reducing Africans to "negroes" was an ideological and semantic normalcy for centuries in European and English languages. The "yellow peril" had resulted in the dispersion of the Japanese people into concentration camps. Colour, ethnicity and bodies had long been conflated with moral/ cultural ontologies. It is not an exaggeration to say that it was within the context and content of these practices, meanings and political possibilities that the liberal multicultural construction of woman of colour took place. Its epistemological pivot rests on the seemingly benign concept of diversity, a re-named version of plurality, so central to the concept and politics of liberalism. This positivity which is implied in the ideology of diversity mitigates the revulsion that women might feel towards calling themselves or others women of colour. A colour coded self-perception, an identity declared on the semiological basis of one's skin colour, was rendered palatable through this ideology of diversity. Our colour provided the sovereign mark, significant enough to be used as a counter in the political discourse of liberalism. As with all liberal pluralist projects, this constituent element of political identities of others did not come up for scrutiny or a critique, but rather became a given, common sensical category of representation, as though always already there. Moreover, the word "colour" became an associational and connotative path to diverse histories and cultures of the nations of other women. They themselves summoned it to convey their colourfulness through it, thereby quickly slipping into the cultural discourse of tradition versus modernity. Their colour signalled traditional cultures, in a constellation of invented traditions.[8] Culturally integrated colour was thus seemingly divested of its racist undertones, and lost its location in power relations. This erasure indicates the epistemological possibilities of the notion of multicultural diversity. If this desocialized and ahistorical notion of diversity were not a naturalized form of political culture and discourse in Canada, and in the West as a whole, such a coinage or neologism would not have been so easily adopted by women who see themselves as practitioners of politics of opposition. The formal equality of liberal pluralism encoded by diversity also helped to allay anxieties and suspicions.

It may be objected that I am making a mountain out of a mole hill by focusing so much on one single political and cultural expression. Does a name, it may be asked, make so much difference? Would not a rose by any other name smell as sweet? If we had instead called ourselves non-white women, for example, what different political task would we have accomplished? My answer to these anticipated objections or questions would be that the language with which we build or express our political agency has to be taken very seriously. An expression in that context, even when it seems innocuous and solitary, has to be treated as a bit of ideology, and as a part of a broader ideological semantics called discourse. Thus we have to treat woman of colour as a name for a particular type of political agency and examine its ability to disclose our lives and experiences as lived within an organization of social relations of power. It is only then that we can attend to the political direction to which this agency points us. Treated thus, we can safely say that the notion woman of colour does not direct us to examine crucial social relations within which we live, to histories and forms of consciousness of power that mark our presence in the U.S. or Canada. Instead this, as a naturalized reworking of coloured woman, performs an ideological accommodation of "race," while erasing class. Also, in thus equating our political identities with a racialized cultural construction, a second level of reality is created which is far from the actualities of our lives. Yet these social actualities are the realities that need to be daily addressed and changed through our politics. If, at least in the course of our antiracist feminist politics, we call ourselves non-white women, we can gesture towards white privilege. The use of a negative prefix automatically raises issues and questions. But a substitution through the language of diversity and colour distracts us from what actually happens to us in our raced and gendered class existence and culturalizes our politics. In other words, it depoliticizes us.[9]

Since the responsibility for this depoliticization falls upon the epistemology and ideology of diversity, the cornerstone of a pluralist liberal politics and its legitimation, we need to explore extensively and critically the workings of the concept of diversity. Official multiculturalism, which has also become the politics of Canadian civil society, our daily political commonsense, cannot be challenged otherwise. The political culture generated by the state in its reflexive dependence on everyday social culture cannot be kept insulated from the ongoing life of the civil society. If resistance politics develops from below, from the civil society, and if that realm itself is saturated with an historical and official political culture of domination, then that politics of resistance itself can become a part of the state's ideological apparatus. The dangers inherent in constructing a multicultural Canada, with a reified and racialized political agency called woman of colour, calls for a critique of the epistemology and ideology of diversity. The next section of this paper, therefore, engages in this critique, and takes up diversity which endows its discursive affiliates, such as woman of colour, with the power to erase or empty out actual social relations and forms of power — "race," gender and class — while creating an aura of concreteness or meaning whose actual relevances or coordinates are located within the state's discourse of ruling.

THE NAME OF THE ROSE, OR WHAT DIFFERENCE DOES IT MAKE WHAT I CALL IT

Diversity has become a commonplace word in our political and cultural world. This seems to have happened in the last decade or so — it has sort of crept up on us. So much so that even businesses have adapted their talk about profit and productivity to the language of diversity, while governments and public institutions set up bureaucracies in its name. On our side, that is, on the side of the people, from below, organizations have been created merging notions of community with diversity — speaking to ethno-cultural pluralities and collective cultural identities. We have versions of this in our everyday language, and in that of scholarship. We have critical feminist anthologies of the politics of diversity,[10] while political theorists have used the term in their communitarian and liberal ways (Eliott & Fleras, 1992; Kymlicka, 1995; Taylor, 1992, 1993; Trudeau, 1968).

So it seems that the time has come to take this rather banal notion of diversity and explore its current popularity in terms of what it does for us politically. To begin with, this word has been used to signify a multiplicity of socio-cultural presences, as a cornucopia of differences of all sorts, that mark the Canadian social space. But this purely descriptive use of the term, signalling heterogeneity without implied power relations, ulterior aim or use, is not the only, or the main, use that has been made of it. This simple descriptive, at most designatory use has been a device for constructing an ideological cultural language or discourse that allows for an instant jump from description to political meanings and practices.

This discourse of diversity is a fusion of a cultural classification, or an empirical/descriptive gesture, with politics. That is, our empirically being from various countries, with our particular looks, languages and cultures, has become an occasion for interpreting, constructing and ascribing differences with connotations of power relations. This process and its conceptual products combine into a political discourse and related ideological practices. In this political deployment the notion of diversity escapes from its denotative function and dictionary meaning and emerges as a value-free, power neutral indicator of difference and multiplicity. But this very character and claim of neutrality allows it to become the governing concept of a complex discourse of social power with its own and related webs of concepts. There is a process of surpassing as well as of subsumption involved in this creation of an ideology from the notion of diversity. Conceived as discourse diversity is not a simple descriptive affair. As a centre piece of a discourse of power and as a device for social management of inequality, it is simultaneously interpretive or meaning-making and actively practical. It creates and mediates practices, both conceptual and actual, of power — of ruling or governing.[11] In this discursive mode the concept of diversity entails two functions, which together allow it to be articulated or bonded with other political notions and practices already in place. Together with them, such as with feminism or antiracism, they form a conceptual network and signal to ideological practices of socio-political administration which are certainly not value neutral.

The two ways in which the neutral appearance of the notion of diversity becomes a useful ideology to practices of power are quite simple. On the one hand, the use of such a concept with a reference to simple multiplicity allows the reading of all social and cultural forms or differences in terms of descriptive plurality. On the other, in its relationship to description it introduces the need to put in or retain a concrete, particular content for each of these seemingly neutral differences. The social relations of power that create the difference implied in sexist-racism, for example, just drop out of sight, and social being becomes a matter of a cultural essence (Bannerji, 1991). This is its paradox — that the concept of diversity simultaneously allows for an emptying out of actual social relations and suggests a concreteness of cultural description, and through this process obscures any understanding of difference as a construction of power. Thus there is a construction of a collective cultural essence and a conflation of this, or what we are culturally supposed to be, and what we are ascribed with, in the context of social organization of inequality. We cannot then make a distinction between racist stereotypes and ordinary historical/cultural differences of everyday life and practices of people from different parts of the world. Cultural traits that come, let us say, from different parts of the third world are used to both create and eclipse racism, and we are discouraged from reading them in terms of relations and symbolic forms of power. The result is also an erasure of class and patriarchy among the immigrant multi-cultures of others, as they too fall within this paradox of essentialization and multiplicity signified by cultural diversity of official multiculturalism. In fact, it is this uncritical, de-materialized, seemingly de-politicized reading of culture through which culture becomes a political tool, an ideology of power which is expressed in racist-sexist or heterosexist differences. One can only conclude from all this that the discourse of diversity, as a complex systemically interpretive language of governing, cannot be read as an innocent pluralism.[12]

The ideological nature of this language of diversity is evident from its frequent use and efficacy in the public and official, that is, institutional realms. In these contexts its function has been to provide a conceptual apparatus in keeping with needs which the presence of heterogeneous peoples and cultures has created in the Canadian state and public sphere. This has both offset and, thus, stabilized the Canadian national imaginary[13] and its manifestation as the state apparatus, which is built on core assumptions of cultural and political homogeneity of a Canadianness. This language of diversity is a coping mechanism for dealing with an actually conflicting heterogeneity, seeking to incorporate it into an ideological binary which is predicated upon the existence of a homogeneous national, that is, a Canadian cultural self with its multiple and different others (see Bannerji, 1997). These multiple other cultural presences in Canada, interpreted as a threat to national culture which called for a coping, and therefore for an incorporating and interpretive mechanism, produced the situation summed up as the challenge of multiculturalism. This has compelled administrative, political and ideological innovations which will help to maintain the status quo. This is where the discourse of diversity has been of crucial importance because this new language of ruling and administration protects ideologies and practices already in place. It is postulated upon pluralist premises of a liberal democratic state, which Canada aspires to be, but also adds specific dimensions of legitimation to particular administrative functions.[14]

The usefulness of the discourse of diversity as a device for managing public or social relations and spaces, of serving as a form of moral regulation of happy co-existence, is obvious. The Canadian government and other public institutions, the media, and the ideological projection of the Canadian nation (and its unity) are marked by this discourse. In the universities, both in pedagogic and administrative spheres, this language is prominent. It is the staple discourse of arts and community projects, conditioning their working agendas as well as the politics of the funding bodies. In workplaces diversity sensitization or training has largely displaced talk about and/or resistance to racism and sexism. Even law appeals to diversity in using cultural and religious defences, suppressing contradictions and violences of patriarchy, for example, while fulfilling the state's pluralist obligations (see Volpp, 1994). In the context of making the Canadian nation, unity is posited in terms of diversity, with pictures of many facial types, languages and cultures — "together we are ...."[15] It is not surprising that Benetton produces a diversity slogan of "united colours" to capture its multicultural markets.

The discourse of diversity has also inscribed our social movements — the women's movement or the trade union movement, for example — where again it helps to obscure deeper/ structural relations of power, such as of racism and sexism or racist heterosexism,[16] both among women and the working class, and reduces the problem of social justice into questions of curry and turban. Thus social movements share crucial ideological assumptions of those whom they seek to fight and supposedly have political differences with. In this regard it is important to do a brief retrospective on the issue of difference within feminist theorization and the women's movement. The issue of "race" in particular became one issue of contention.

Many years ago Elizabeth Spelman (1988) wrote a book criticizing North American liberal/bourgeois feminism for its Eurocentrism. Her book, entitled *Inessential Woman: Problems of Exclusion in Feminist Thought*, created disturbing resonances in the world of North American anglophone feminist theories, and many of us used her critique to get a clarity on our own dissatisfaction about mainstream feminism. This critique of essentialism and Eurocentrism, which I addressed in "But Who Speaks for Us" (Bannerji, 1991), developed into a critique of an ideological and identity stance known as whiteness. The most well-known form of this notion is in Ruth Frankenberg's *White Women, Race Matters: The Social Construction of Whiteness* (1993). Though various critiques and adjustments were made of Spelman's and Frankenberg's theorizations and politics, their articulations remain powerful even as they, as white women, confront other white women and speak as insiders to that social ontology. Many others, including Ann Laura Stoler (1995), wrote on various ideological and political aspects of whiteness. However, as Leslie Roman (1993, p. 72) says:

> ... to say that white is a color does not rescue the concept of "race" from similar forms of empty pluralism and dangerous relativism invoked by the larger essentialist discourse of "race". Try as I might to recognize whiteness as a structural power relation that confers cultural and economic privileges, the phrase, spoken declaratively by the racially privileged, can also become a form of white defensiveness.

But of more immediate importance for us are the critiques made by black and third world feminists, such as Collins, Mohanty and Alexander, regarding the politically exclusionary, debilitating and epistemologically occlusive effects of such theorization as conducted within the academy. In their anthology Alexander and Mohanty especially take to task women's studies within U.S. academies. Even among those who claim oppositional knowledge and practices, they declared, "the color of our gender mattered" (Alexander & Mohanty, 1997, p. xiv). They were, they stated, neither "the right color" nor gender, nor nationality in terms of self-definition of the U.S. academy, and by extension of the women's studies establishment (p. xiv). Alexander and Mohanty broaden their critical outreach and compare this outsider status in institutions of learning to the citizenship machinery and ideology deployed in the U.S. The outsider or the alien is born both within the U.S. and outside of its national territories. As they put it (p. xiv): "Our experience makes sense only in analogy to African-American women." The authors in this anthology also question the political and epistemological impact that postmodernism is having within women's studies. As Mohanty and Alexander see it (p. xvii), "... in its haste to dissociate itself from all forms of essentialism, [this impact] has generated a series of epistemological confusions regarding the interconnections between location, identity and construction of knowledge." This refusal of experience, history, and identity in its broadest sense of self-recovery, often found in the curricula of women's studies, has delegitimized the type of grounded social knowledge spoken of by Collins in her two books. The organic intellectuals of the oppressed become invalid by definition if they can not claim their lives as sources for learning and theorizing, as exemplars for the unjust relations within which they live. As Mohanty and Alexander put it (p. xvii): "... localized questions of experience, identity, culture and history, which enable us to understand specific processes of domination and subordination, are often dismissed by postmodern theories as reiteration of cultural 'essences,' or unified stable identity." These current critiques were anticipated as early as 1982 by Hazel Carby (1982).

This discourse of diversity in its comprehensive ideological and political form is materialized and extended as the discourse of multiculturalism, with its linguistic constellation of visible minority, women of colour and so on. Cultural sensitivity towards and tolerance of others (to the core/national culture and agency) are two behavioural imperatives of this multicultural politics, both at the level of state and society. The all-pervasive presence of diversity in our public discourse has created a situation where even those who are not entirely comfortable with its discursive constellation use it in its various guises in an unconscious submission to what is around, and for reasons of intelligibility. Being effective with funding proposals means translating our needs and concerns into the discourses of multiculturalism. This means speaking in the language of cultural communities and their diversities, of ethnicities and women of colour and visible minorities — both male and female. Otherwise our funders or the state do not hear us.

So, it would seem that there is much invested in the fact of naming, in the words we use to express our socio-political understandings, because they are more than just words, they are ideological concepts. They imply intentions and political and organizational practices. Calling people by different names, in different political contexts, has always produced significantly different results. These names are, after all, not just names to call people by, but rather codes for political subjectivities and agencies. Naming ourselves in terms of class, for example as the proletariat, assuming class as the basis of our political identity, would imply a different political ideology, practice and goal, than if we constructed our political agency with names such as women/people of colour or visible minorities. Contrary to Shakespeare's assertion that a rose by any other name would smell as sweet, we see that not to be the case in political-ideological matters. In politics the essence of the flower lies in the name by which it is called. In fact it is the naming that decides what flower we have at hand. To say this is to say explicitly that discourse is more than a linguistic manoeuvre. It is a matter of putting in words, mediating and organizing social relations of ruling, of meanings organized through power. It is best to remind ourselves of the title of Dionne Brand's poetry book, *No Language is Neutral* (1990).

THE ESSENCE OF THE NAME, OR WHAT IS TO BE GAINED BY CALLING SOMETHING DIVERSITY

In order to understand how the concept of diversity works ideologically, we have to feed into it the notion of difference constructed through social relations of power and read it in terms of the binaries of homogeneity and heterogeneity already referred to in our discussion on multiculturalism. It does not require much effort to realize that diversity is not equal to multiplied sameness, rather it presumes a distinct difference in each instance. But this makes us ask, distinctly different from what? The answer is, obviously, from each other and from whatever it is that is homogeneous — which is an identified and multiplied sameness, serving as the distinguishing element at the core in relation to which difference is primarily measured. The difference that produces heterogeneity suggests otherness in relation to that core, and in social politics this otherness is more than an existential, ontological fact. It is a socially constructed otherness or heterogeneity, its difference signifying both social value and power. It is not just another cultural self floating non-relationally in a socio-historical vacuum. In the historical context of the creation of Canada, of its growth into an uneasy amalgam of a white settler colony with liberal democracy, with its internally colonized or peripheral economies, the definitions and relations between a national self and its other, between homogeneity and heterogeneity, sameness and diversity, become deeply power ridden.[17] From the days of colonial capitalism to the present-day global imperialism, there has emerged an ideologically homogeneous identity dubbed Canadian whose nation and state Canada is supposed to be.

This core community is synthesized into a national we, and it decides on the terms of multiculturalism and the degree to which multicultural others should be tolerated or accommodated. This "we" is an essentialized version of a colonial European turned into Canadian and the subject or the agent of Canadian nationalism. It is this essence, extended to the notion of a community, that provides the point of departure for the ideological deployment of diversity. The practice is clearly exclusive, not only of third world or non-white ethnic immigrants, but also of the aboriginal population.[18] Though often described in cultural linguistic terms as the two nations of anglophones and francophones, the two nations theory does not include non-whites of these same language groups. So the identity of the Canadian "we" does not reside in language, religion or other aspects of culture, but rather in the European/North American physical origin — in the body and the colour of skin. Colour of skin is elevated here beyond its contingent status and becomes an essential quality called whiteness, and this becomes the ideological signifier of a unified non-diversity.[19] The others outside of this moral and cultural whiteness are targets for either assimilation or toleration. These diverse or multicultural elements, who are also called newcomers, introducing notions of territoriality and politicized time, create accommodational difficulties for white

Canadians, both at the level of the civil society, of culture and economy, and also for the ruling practices of the state. An ideological coping mechanism becomes urgent in view of a substantial third world immigration allowed by Canada through the 1960s up to recent years (see Eliott & Fleras, 1992). This new practical and discursive/ideological venture, or an extension of what Althusser has called an ideological state apparatus, indicates both the crisis and its management. After all, the importation of Chinese or South Asian indentured labour, or the legally restricted presence of the Japanese since the last century, did not pose the same problems which the newly arrived immigrants do (see Bolaria & Li, 1988). As landed residents or apprentice citizens, or as actual citizens of Canada, they cannot be left in the same limbo of legal and political non-personhood as their predecessors were until the 1950s. Yet they are not authentic Canadians in the ideological sense, in their physical identity and culture. What is more, so-called authentic Canadians are unhappy with their presence, even though they enhance Canada's economic growth. Blue ribbon Hong Kong immigrants, for example, bring investments which may be needed for the growth of British Columbia, but they themselves are not wanted.[20] But they, among other third world immigrants, are here, and this calls for the creation of an ideology and apparatus of multiculturalism (with its discourse of a special kind of plurality called diversity) as strategies of containment and management.

If this statement seems to be unfounded, we need only note the time around which multiculturalism and the diversity discourse is invented in Canada. Multi-ethnic European immigrations of the past did not inspire it, nor are the present-day European immigrants the targets of this discourse, even though cultural, religious, and linguistic differences are very high between them and the two nations of anglo- and francophone communities. An unspoken but active melting pot stance pretty much seems to have been in place. We began to hear of the notion of diversity from the time of allowing citizenship to the previously indentured Chinese and South Asians, from the time of Canada's open door policy in relation to its plans for capitalist growth. The metaphor of Canadian society as the vertical mosaic is an early intimation of the complexities of evolution of a political ideology involving otherness in a liberal democratic context. The open door policy not only allowed but actively pursued immigration from ex-colonized third world countries. Along with that came political refugees. This is when diversity came to be seen as really diverse, in spite of the fact that many came from French and English speaking countries, many were christians, and a large number had more than a passing acquaintance with cultures of Europe and North America. But as they were not indentured workers, or for the most part not illegals, their presence as workers, taxpayers and electoral constituencies was a force to be reckoned with and a problem to be managed. The multicultural policy had to be evolved and put in place for them.

The Canadian state had to deal with a labour importation policy which was primarily meant to create a working class, but not guest workers as in Germany. This involved resistance from white Canadians, from the so-called Canadian worker. It also had to contain the mobility drives of immigrants who were otherwise compliant, but wanted to get a secure economic niche in the country's labour and consumer markets. In the very early 1980s Prime Minister Pierre Trudeau enunciated his multicultural policy, and a discourse of nation, community and diversity began to be cobbled together. There were no strong multicultural demands on the part of third world immigrants themselves to force such a policy. The issues raised by them were about racism, legal discrimination involving immigration and family reunification, about job discrimination on the basis of Canadian experience, and various adjustment difficulties, mainly of child care and language. In short, they were difficulties that are endemic to migration, and especially that of people coming in to low income jobs or with few assets. Immigrant demands were not then, or even now, primarily cultural, nor was multiculturalism initially their formulation of the solution to their problems. It began as a state or an official/institutional discourse, and it involved the translation of issues of social and economic injustice into issues of culture (see Kymlicka 1995). Often it was immigrant questions and quandaries *vis a vis* the response of the so-called Canadians that prompted justificatory gestures by the state. These legitimation gestures were more directed at the discontented Canadians than the discriminated others. Multiculturalism was therefore not a demand from below, but an ideological elaboration from above in which the third world immigrants found themselves. This was an apparatus which rearranged questions of social justice, of unemployment and racism, into issues of cultural diversity and focused on symbols of religion, on so-called tradition. Thus immigrants were ethnicized, culturalized and mapped into traditional/ethnic communities. Gradually a political and administrative framework came into being where structural inequalities could be less and less seen or spoken about. Antiracism and class politics could not keep pace with constantly proliferating ideological state or institutional apparatuses which identified people in terms of their cultural identity, and converted or conflated racist ascriptions of difference within the Canadian space into the power neutral notion of diversity. An increase in threats against third world immigrants, the rise of neo-nazi white supremacist groups and ultra conservative politics, along with a systemic or structural racism and anti-immigration and anti-immigrant stances of political parties, could now be buried or displaced as the immigrants' own cultural problem. Politics in Canada were reshaped and routed through this culturalization or ethnicization, and a politics of identity was constructed which the immigrants themselves embraced as the only venue for social and political agency.

Now it was projected to the world at large that what the incoming third world population of Canada primarily wanted was the same religious, linguistic and cultural life they had in their countries of origin. They were frozen into being seen as traditional cultures and thus socially conservative in entirety. They were bringing down the standards of Canadian modernity and criminalizing the country. The problem for the Canadian state and society then became one of considering what or how much they could retain in Canada of their previous cultures without compromising the national character. The fact that their demands came in many types, and the most important ones pertained to discrimination by the state and the economy which threatened worthwhile employment possibilities, family re-unification for refugees, facilities for women, and so forth, became political non-issues. This emphasis on culture, on immigrants' ethnic self-definition and fundamentalist cultural survivalism, deflected proper publicization and criticism of police violence or general safety issues for non-white people, especially for black youth.[21] In almost every case of police shooting, the police were given immunity, and immigration laws became tighter while deportations increasingly became a threat. De-skilling, not just through underemployment or unemployment, but through state/institutional decertification of professionals, is also a basic fact of third world immigrant lives (see Bolaria & Li, 1988, p. 18; Government of Canada, 1986; Government of Canada, 1984). No third world immigrant is left in doubt that he/she is in Canada on public and official sufferance and is to be grateful for being allowed into the country. They are made to feel that otherness is of an antagonistic variety to Canadians, and they also know that this otherness is not in them, but in how they are perceived, what ascriptions pre-exist their arrival into the country, how racialization and ethnicization have already put a white Canada in place. They come to know that they are seen as virtually invading this Canada. It becomes quickly evident that in a society that preaches the gospel of wealth, they would not and are not expected to go very far. They judge by their presences and absences in the social and economic spaces that they are here to primarily reproduce the under classes.

Through the decades from the 1960s political developments took place in Canada which show the twists and turns in the relationship between third world immigrants and the state.[22] With the disarray of left politics in the country and growth of multicultural ideology, all political consciousness regarding third world immigrants has been multiculturalized. These cultural/ethnicized formulations were like chemical probes into a test tube of solution around which dissatisfactions and mobility drives of the others began to coalesce. Wearing or not wearing of turbans, publicly funded heritage language classes, state supported islamic schools modelled on the existence and patterns of catholic schools, for example, provided the profile of their politics. They themselves often forgot how much less important these were than their full citizenship rights, their demand for jobs, non-discriminatory schools and work places, and a generally non-racist society. Differentiated second or third class citizenships evolved, as a non-white sub-working class continued to develop. Their initial willingness to work twice as hard to get a little never materialized into much. Instead a mythology developed around their lack of success, which spoke of their shifty, lazy work habits and their scamming and unscrupulous use of the welfare system. This is especially ironic since they often came from countries, such as those in the West Indies, from which Canada continues to bring substantial profits. But this story of neo-colonialism, of exploitation, racism, discrimination and hierarchical citizenship never gains much credibility or publicity with the Canadian state, the public or the media. This reality is what the cultural language and politics of diversity obscures, displaces and erases. It is obvious that the third world or non-white immigrants are not the beneficiaries of the discourse of diversity.

The state of Canada wants its differentiated inferior citizens to speak in the state's own language of multicultural identity, of ethnicity and community. This is mainly the language of representation permitted to them. Ethnic or racialized cultural community, not political community organized on the basis of class, gender and racialization, is what the state is willing to acknowledge in their case. Continuous struggles involving issues of "race" and class have created something called "race" relations in some institutions, which, if it becomes antiracist in any real way, is de-scaled or defunded. Human Rights Commissions, treating cases individually, with no proper powers of enforcement, often act as pawns of the state and capital, adjudicate very few cases and rule rarely in favour of the complainant. Ritualistic non-discrimination clauses that are at times present in state documents to mediate "race" relations often create the impression that "races" actually exist as biological social entities determining behaviour and culture, and only need to relate better. There is not even a language within the state's redress apparatus to capture or describe the racist sexism towards third world or non-white women or men. By simultaneously blocking the politico-social process of racialization from view while organizing people as raced ethnicities, the state of multiculturalism seeks to obscure issues of class and patriarchy as actionable, and therefore the possibility of discovering inter-community commonalities — for example between third world immigrants and aboriginal peoples, or among the different strands of working classes — diminishes considerably.

Multiculturalism as an official practice and discourse has worked actively to create the notion and practices of insulated communities. Under its political guidance and funding a political-social space was organized. Politically constructed homogenized communities, with their increasingly fundamentalist boundaries of cultures, traditions and religions, emerged from where there were immigrants from different parts of the world with different cultures and values. They developed leaders or spokespersons, usually men, who liaised with the state on their behalf, and their organizational behaviour fulfilled the expectations of the Canadian state. New political agents and constituencies thus came to life, as people sought to be politically active in these new cultural identity terms. So they became interpellated by the state under certain religious and ethnically named agencies. Hardheaded businessmen, who had never thought of culture in their lives before, now, upon entering Canada, began using this notion and spoke to the powers that be in terms of culture and welfare of their community. But this was the new and only political playing field for "others" in Canada, a slim opportunity of mobility, so they were/are willing to run through the multicultural maze. What is more, this new cultural politics, leaving out problems of class and patriarchy, appealed to the conservative elements in the immigrant population, since religion could be made to overdetermine these uncomfortable actualities, and concentrated on the so-called culture and morality of the community. Official multiculturalism, which gave the conservative male self-styled representatives *carte blanche* to do this, also empowered the same male leaders as patriarchs and enhanced their sexism and masculinism. In the name of culture and god, within the high walls of community and ethnicity, women and children could be dominated and acted against violently because the religions or culture and tradition of others supposedly sanctioned this oppression and brutality. And as politically and ideologically constituted homogenized cultural essences which are typed as traditional, such as muslim or sikh or hindu communities, violence against women could go on without any significant or effective state intervention.

For these newly constructed communities, which came to life from scattered populations of the world and based their tenuous cohesion on a minimal doctrinaire affiliation (such as the hindu religion, for example), a heterosexist world view and mistrust of class politics, the multicultural dispensations of the state were a fortunate intervention. Their ethnic self-appellations, born of their long familiarity with colonial and imperialist discourse, were perfectly in keeping with colonial-racist stereotypes used by the Canadian state and culture. It was and is not noted either by the multicultural state or its clients, the so-called communities, that back in their so-called home countries, in whose names their multiculture is fabricated, the contestation that is going on bears little resemblance to these monolithic identities that they project in Canada. Being real countries, lived historical political spaces, these countries were and are going through many political and social struggles, changing their forms, none of which were in a position to be petrified into immutable cultural identities.[23] The genealogies of these reified cultural identities which are mobilized in Canada are entirely colonial, though they are being constantly re-worked in the modern context of state formation and capital's transformation. In fact the earlier European orientalist racist perceptions of India, for example, perfectly tally with the Canadian state's and the media's perception of the Indian communities in Canada.[24] The concept of tradition is the principle of continuity and serves as the interpretive and constructive category in both cases. A simple binary of cultural stereotyping of tradition and modernity stands for India and Canada, respectively. The problem of multiculturalism, then, is how much tradition can be accommodated by Canadian modernity without affecting in any real way the overall political and cultural hegemony of Europeans. It is also assumed by both the state and the media, as well as the male representatives of the communities, that Indians or South Asians are essentially traditional and as such patriarchy is congenial to their cultural identity, while class conflict is a modern or non-traditional aberration.

The result of this convergence between the Canadian state and conservative male representatives or community agents has been very distressing for women in particular. Between the multicultural paradigm and the actuality of a migrant citizen's life in Canada, the gap is immense. Among multiculturalists of both the communitarian and the liberal persuasion Canada is a nation space which contains different "races" and ethnicities, and this presence demands either a "politics of recognition" (Taylor, 1992) or a modified set of individual and group rights. But for both groups this diversity of others or difference between Canadian self and other has no political dimension. It speaks to nothing like class formation or class struggle, of the existence of active and deep racism, or of a social organization entailing racialized class production of gender. The history of colonization is also not brought to bear on the notions of diversity and difference. So, the answer to my original question — what is to be gained from a discourse of diversity and its politics of multiculturalism? — lies in just what has actually happened in Canadian politics and its theorization, what I have been describing so far, namely in the erasure and occlusion of social relations of power and ruling. This diversified reification of cultures and culturalization of politics allows for both the practice and occlusion of heterosexism and racism of a narrow bourgeois nationalism. This means the maintenance of a status quo of domination. Many hard socio-political questions and basic structural changes may now be avoided. People can be blamed for bringing on their own misfortunes, while rule of capital and class can continue their violence of racism, sexism and homophobia.

CONCLUSION

It should be obvious by now that diversity discourse portrays society as a horizontal space, in which there is no theoretical or analytical room for social relations of power and ruling, of socio-economic contradictions that construct and regulate Canadian political economy and its ideological culture. Yet the very need to formulate notions of multiculturalism and diversity, and their introjection into politics and state formation, into the very modes of governance, indicates that all is not as harmonious as it should be. The presence of certain peoples in the Canadian socio-economic and cultural spaces has obviously been considered exceptional, unusual or irregular. Yet their presence has also called into question much of what has been considered usual or regular. This has meant initiating a degree of adjustment for the majority communities and their state which, while sidestepping existing ideological practices, has meant the invention of this ideological state apparatus and cultural language of multiculturalism.

But the discourse of diversity is not new or *sui generis*. As I mentioned before, it is derived from and is in keeping with a language of plurality that has existed in liberal democracy. It relies, as we saw, on reading the notion of difference in a socially abstract manner, which also wipes away its location in history, thus obscuring colonialism, capital and slavery. It displaces these political and historical readings by presenting a complex interpretive code which encapsulates a few particularities of people's cultures, adding a touch of reality, and averts our gaze from power relations or differences which continue to organize the Canadian public life and culture. They assert themselves as perceptions of otherness encoding a hegemonic European-Canadianness.

As I have shown above, by obscuring or deflecting from historical and present power relations, perceptions and systematized ideologies, the deployment of diversity reduces to and manages difference as ethnic cultural issues. It then becomes a matter of co-existence of value-free, power-neutral plurality, of cultural differences where modernity and tradition, so-called white and black cultures, supposedly hold the same value. That is, diversity discourse tries to set up a sphere which claims to be outside of hegemony. It does so uncritically, unreflexively, and yet cannot escape the role of being an instrument of designation of some cultures as *real* culture, while others fall into the category of sub-culture and multiculture, cultures of the peripheries. This is not dissonant with colonial anthropology's way of assigning non-European cultures a special, hyphenated and bracketed status.[25] This way of thinking accomplishes depoliticization at deeply complex conceptual and political levels. Simultaneously as it disarticulates culture from hegemony, it reduces all political issues into cultural ones and converts culture into a private matter. This removes the civil society — its politically charged expressions, ways of being and seeing, what Gramsci called social common sense — from being considered as the soil and the material for political formations and articulation. This process in effect transforms the category culture into a practical device which both erases and stands in for the social. Any materialist dialectic of culture is dispensed with.[26]

This conceptual feat of emptying out difference of its actual political and cultural content, and thus presenting it as neutral diversity, can only be done by relying on the wholly artificial separation of the public and the private — as parallels of the political and the personal. It is possible because the concept of diversity is much more hospitable to an abstract notion of plurality than that of difference, which instantly summons questions of comparison to others with regard to whom any difference is postulated. A socialization, and therefore politicization, of this concept of difference is far more likely than diversity to lend itself to content saturated with social relations of class, gender, "race," sexuality and so on. This makes difference a much better heuristic device, if not exactly an analytical concept, for understanding situations which both imply and call for politics. We might at this point ask, how we should name ourselves, or what would be an effective name for capturing the oppositional thrust of our political agency? Though it is not possible for me to provide an answer which would satisfy all feminists, nor is it my intention to do so, this topic of named agency and its subjectivity demands a greater clarification. I am content to call myself an antiracist and marxist feminist. It is a distinctly political and socially grounded cultural identity. It does not rely solely on the culture of community at birth, but also speaks to what we have become as political subjects and agents in our own adult political and cultural efforts. This striving for a political self-definition, a self-conscious anti-oppression task of historical recovery, is not a matter of essentialized cultural diversities, but rather, as Paula Moya says (Alexander and Mohanty, 1997, p. 141), it involves an act of "deconstruction of difference." With class, "race" and gender and sexuality seen as components of this difference, we admit of both solidarities and relations of opposition. We can unite, as coalition is a basic prerequisite of organizing for change, with others inhabiting similar socio-cultural locations, and see that unity in political terms. This seeing of common social conditions produced through oppressive relations, rather than an essentialized version of cultures, is an act and task of political conscientization. This admits of asymmetrical social and cultural locations and power relations (for example, between straight and lesbian non-white women in North America), while also moving toward a new level of political consciousness and a culture of resistance. This culture also exists historically with us, as our legacy.

This same question of political naming, or agency, has been discussed by many feminists, white and non-white. For Mohanty and Alexander, the answer lies in democracy, but not of the capitalist liberal type. They evolve the notion of feminist democracy, but feminist distinct from radical feminism. They speak (1997, pp. xxix-xxxi) to a "transborder, transnational participatory democracy" which resists hegemonic democracy of our times, and to "universal citizenship," to "anticapitalist, anticolonial feminist democracy" in a very similar way to my proposal. This is not radical democracy without class, class struggle or anti-imperialism. Thus it is different from the projects for new social movements as enunciated by Ernesto Laclau and Chantal Mouffe and their followers, who believe that they can make democracy real without fighting racialized gendered, local, national and global capitalism. Alexander and Mohanty eschew cultural relativism encouraged by multiculturalism from above, and seek a redefinition of justice. They want to see a "critical application of feminist praxis in global contexts" which insists on "responsibility, accountability, engagement and solidarity," and advance in their anthology "a paradigm of decolonization which stresses power, history, memory, relational analysis, justice (not just representation), and ethics as the issues central to [their] analysis of globalization." (1997, p. xix) I would say this is a proposal which we should support as the most extensively liberatory one.

But as things are at present, people are not doing a politics consistent with my proposal. We continue to subscribe to the discourse of diversity or liberal plurality, forgetting both its de-politicizing capacity and its ability to perform a most powerful political function. We might remind ourselves what the political cognates of diversity are. We might ask what is its home discourse, for concepts do have homes in a general discursive constellation, and what are their ideological-political imports? The discursive home and political cognates of diversity lie in liberal democracy, whose particular ways of constructing a self-enclosed, self-sustaining polity through the mechanism of installing a separation between the state and the civil society, and the reduction of equality into a formal gesture, have long been noted (see McPherson, 1977). This is the meaning of the concept of citizenship in liberal or bourgeois democracy, which rests on divesting the political from the social, the equality of citizenship from the inequality of class and other power relations. The so-called diverse cultural or ethnic communities are also constructed on this model as equal to each other and to the dominant Canadian culture of Euro-Americans. Diversity relies on the postulation of an abstracted, non-social ground zero.

Diversity as discourse, with its constellation of concepts such as multiculturalism, ethnicity, community, and so forth, becomes an important way in which the abstract or formal equality of liberal democracy, its empty pluralism, can gain a concreteness or an embodiment. Through it the concept of citizenship rids itself of its emptiness and takes on signals of a particularized social being or a cultural personhood. The sameness implied in the liberal notion citizenship is then stencilled onto a so-called diverse culture, and offers a sense of concrete specificity. This purported plurality with pseudo-concreteness rescues class democracy, and does not let the question of power relations get out of hand. Differences or diversities are then seen as inherent, as ontological or cultural traits of the individuals of particular cultural communities, rather than as racist ascriptions or stereotypes. This helps the cause of the status quo and maintains ascribed and invented ethnicities, or their displaced and intensified communal forms. The discourse of diversity makes it impossible to understand or name systemic and cultural racism, and its implication in gender and class.

When concreteness or embodiment is thus ideologically depoliticized and dehistoricized by its articulation to the discourse of diversity, we are presented with many ontological cultural particularities which serve as markers of ethnicity and group boundaries. Since these ethnic communities are conceived as discrete entities, and there is no recognition of a core cultural-power group, a dispersion effect is introduced through the discourse of diversity which occludes its own presumption of otherness, of being diverse, and which is predicated upon a homogeneous Canadian identity.

It is with regard to this that diversity is measured, and hides its assumptions of homogeneity under the cover of a value and power neutral heterogeneity. Thus it banishes from view a process of homogenization or essentialization which underpins the project of liberal pluralism.

Ultimately then, the discourse of diversity is an ideology. It has its own political imperatives in what is called multiculturalism elaborated within the precincts of the state. It translates out into different political possibilities within the framework of capitalism and bourgeois democracy, and both communitarian liberals and liberals for individual rights may find it congenial to their own goals. Politics of recognition, an ideology of tolerance, advocacy of limited group rights, may all result from adopting the discourse of diversity, but what difference they would actually make to those people's lives which are objects of multicultural politics, is another story.

NOTES

This is a reworked version of a paper given at Southeastern Women's Studies Association Annual Conference, Athens, Georgia, April 1997. Thanks are due to the Faculty of Educational Studies, University of British Columbia, for the time given to do research for my work as a visiting scholar. I would especially like to thank Professors Leslie Roman and Patricia Vertinsky for their encouragement and support.

1　Wallace is aware of the problems associated with multiculturalism, but supports it in general from a psychoanalytic perspective involving many aspects of self-formation.

2　See in this context Peter McLaren's introduction to *Revolutionary Multiculturalism* (1997), but also Connolly (1995).

3　Regarding the term 'black women' in political usage, see Sudbury (1998, p. 20, fn 1).

4　Sudbury outlines in her introduction the history of these different bids at political identities and their shifts.

5　For a history of immigration in Canada, see Law Union of Ontario (1981).

6　On "race," colour and the Canadian state's immigration policies in the late 19th/early 20th century, see Government of Canada (1974; 1986).

7   See Brand and Carty (1993); also Ng (1993). For an uncritical liberal view, see Government of Canada (1986).

8   On invention of tradition see Hobsbawm and Ranger (1983); also Mani (1989), and Ismail and Jeganathan (1995).

9   On culturalizing politics, see Benjamin (1969).

10 For an example of feminist anthologies using "diversity" in the title, see Hamilton (1986), especially the introduction.

11 On ideological categories and conceptual practices of power and relations of ruling, see the first two chapters of Smith (1990).

12 For the ground of a theoretical critique of diversity, see Roman (1993).

13 On the Canadian national imaginary see Bannerji (1996).

14 For diversity language in administration, see Davis (1996) on the language of corporate multiculturalism.

15 Common slogan of several government advertising campaigns, to be filled in with "Ontario" or "Canada."

16 For homophobia and racist heterosexism in cultural nationalism or ethnic communitarianism, see, in the U.S. context, Collins (1998) and Carby (1998), to name two texts. In the Canadian context very little has been written about this phenomenon, probably due to the deeply social and economic involvement of the so-called communities in the state's policies of multiculturalism. See Dua and Robertson (1999), especially my paper (Bannerji, 1999).

17 On the racialized nature of Canada's political economy as a white settler colony, and its attempts to retain features of this while installing itself as a liberal democracy, see Bolaria and Li (1988).

18 It is redundant really to speak of the exclusion/marginalization of the aboriginal people in Canada, both in terms of their claim to land and livelihood as well as culture, but the following books are interesting as examples of discussions on these issues. See Kulchyski (1994) and Monture-Angus (1995).

19 On reading the skin as whiteness, as an ideological/political construction, see Frankenburg (1993).

20 On immigration to Canada from Hong Kong, and recent Chinese immigration, see Wong (1997), Li (1993); also Skeldon (1995).

21 Between 1988 and 1992 three unarmed black young men were killed by police in Toronto and one in Montreal, and one young woman permanently paralysed in a police shooting.

22 For example, the change in immigration policy from the "family reunification" programme to a primarily skills based one shifts the demography of Canada.

It brings a kind of immigrant, perhaps from Eastern Europe, who does not pose the problem of "race."

23 See Butalia and Sarkar (1997). The essays in this anthology show the intensity of the political struggle between secular, left feminist forces and the hindu right.

24 An India or South Asia has been invented, with befitting identities or cultural stereotypes for people of the subcontinent living in the diaspora. A production of orientalism and a more forthright racism, these stereotypes rest on the use of the concept of tradition.

25 For examples of colonial anthropology, see Radcliffe-Brown (1965) or Evans-Pritchard (1965); also for its more postmodernist, radical versions, see Geertz (1988) or Comaroff and Comaroff (1991).

26 For a materialist view of culture, see Williams (1980).

REFERENCES

Alarcón, Norma. "Conjugating Subjects in the Age of Multiculturalism." In Avery Gordon and Christopher Newfield, eds. *Mapping Multiculturalism*, 40-48. Minnesota: University of Minnesota Press, 1996.

Alcoff, Linda. "Cultural Feminism versus Post-structuralism: The Identity Crisis in Feminist Theory." *Signs* 13, no. 3 (1988), 405-436.

Alexander, Jacqui, and Chandra Mohanty, eds. *Feminist Genealogies, Colonial Legacies, Democratic Futures*. London and New York: Routledge, 1997.

Althusser, Louis. *Lenin and Philosophy,* trans., Ben Brewster. London: Verso, 1971.

Anthias, Floya, Nira Yuval-Davis, and Harriet Cain, eds. *Racialized Boundaries*. London and New York: Routledge, 1992.

Anzaldúa, Gloria, ed. *Making Face, Making Soul/haciendo caras: Creative and Critical Perspectives by Women of Color*. San Francisco: an aunt lute foundations book, 1990.

Anzaldúa, Gloria, and Cherrie Moraga, eds. *This Bridge Called My Back: Writings by Radical Women of Color*. New York: Kitchen Table Women of Color Press, 1983.

Bannerji, Himani. "But Who Speaks for Us?" In Himani Bannerji, Linda Carty, Kari Dehli, Susan Heald and Kate McKenna, *Unsettling Relations: The University as a Site of Feminist Struggles*, 67-108. Toronto: Women's Press, 1991.

———, ed. *Returning the Gaze: Essays on Racism, Feminism and Politics*. Toronto: Sister Vision Press, 1993.

———. *Thinking Through: Essays on Feminism, Marxism and Antiracism*. Toronto: Women's Press, 1995.

————. "On the Dark Side of the Nation: Politics of Multiculturalism and the State in Canada." *Journal of Canadian Studies* 31, no. 3 (1996), 103-128.

————. "Geography Lessons: On Being an Insider/Outsider to the Canadian Nation." In Leslie Roman and Linda Eyre, eds. *Dangerous Territories: Struggles for Difference and Equality in Education*, 23-42. New York and London: Routledge, 1997.

————. "A Question of Silence: Reflections on Violence against Women in Communities of Colour." In Enakshi Dua and Angela Robertson, eds. *Scratching the Surface: Canadian Anti-racist Feminist Thought*, 261-277. Toronto: Women's Press, 1999.

Benjamin, Walter. "The Work of Art in the Age of Mechanical Reproduction." In *Illuminations*, 217-252. Trans. Harry Zohn. New York: Schocken Books, 1969.

Bhabnani, Kumkum and Ann Phoenix, eds. *Shifting Identities, Shifting Racisms*. London: Sage, 1994.

Brah, Avtar. *Cartographies of Diaspora: Contesting Identities*. London and New York: Routledge, 1996.

Bolaria, B. Singh and Peter S. Li. *Racial Oppression in Canada*. Toronto: Garamond Press, 1988.

Brand, Dionne. *No Language Is Neutral*. Toronto: McClelland and Stewart, 1990.

Brand, Dionne and Linda Carty. "Visible Minority Women: A Creation of the Colonial State." In Himani Bannerji, ed. *Returning the Gaze: Essays on Racism, Feminism and Politics*, 207-222. Toronto: Sister Vision Press, 1993.

Butalia, Urvashi and Tanika Sarkar, eds. *Women of the Hindu Right*. New Delhi: Kali for Women, 1997.

Carby, Hazel V. *Race Men*. Cambridge: Harvard University Press, 1998.

————. "White Women Listen! Black Feminism and the Boundaries of Sisterhood." In Centre for Contemporary Cultural Studies, *The Empire Strikes Back*, 212-235. London: Hutchinson, 1982.

Centre for Contemporary Cultural Studies. *The Empire Strikes Back*. London: Hutchinson, 1982.

Collins, Patricia Hill. *Black Feminist Thought: Knowledge, Consciousness and the Politics of Empowerment*. London: Harper Collins, 1990.

————. *Fighting Words: Black Women and the Search for Justice*. Minneapolis, Minnesota: University of Minnesota Press, 1998.

Comaroff, Jean, and John Comaroff. *Of Revelation and Revolution*. Chicago: University of Chicago Press, 1991.

Connolly, William. *The Ethos of Pluralization*. Minneapolis, Minnesota: University of Minnesota Press, 1995.

Cruz, Jon. "From Farce to Tragedy: Reflections on the Reification of Race at Century's End." In Avery Gordon and Christopher Newfield, eds. *Mapping Multiculturalism*, 19-39. Minneapolis, Minnesota: University of Minnesota Press, 1996.

Davis, Angela Y. "Gender, Class and Multiculturalism: Rethinking 'Race' Politics." In Avery Gordon and Christopher Newfield, eds. *Mapping Multiculturalism*, 40-48. Minnesota: University of Minnesota Press, 1996.

Dua, Ena and Angela Robertson, eds. *Scratching the Surface*. Toronto: Women's Press, 1999.

Eliott, Jean L. and Augie Fleras. *Multiculturalism in Canada: The Challenge of Diversity*. Toronto: Nelson, 1992.

Evans-Pritchard, Edward E. *Theories of Primitive Religion*. Oxford: Clarendon Press, 1965.

Frankenburg, Ruth. *White Women, Race Matters: The Social Construction of Whiteness*. Minneapolis, Minnesota: University of Minnesota Press, 1993.

Geertz, Clifford. *Works and Lives: The Anthropologist as Author*. Stanford, California: Stanford University Press, 1988.

Gilman, Sander. "Black Bodies, White Bodies: Toward an Iconography of Female Sexuality in Late Nineteenth Century Art, Medicine and Literature." In Henry Louis Gates Jr., ed. *"Race" Writing and Difference*, 223-261. Chicago: University of Chicago Press, 1985.

Gilroy, Paul. *Ain't No Black in the Union Jack: The Cultural Politics of Race and Nation*. London: Hutchinson, 1987.

———. *Black Atlantic: Modernity's Double Consciousness*. London: Verso, 1993.

Goldberg, David T., ed. *Multiculturalism: A Critical Reader*. Oxford: Blackwell, 1994.

Gomez-Peña, Guillermo. *The New World Border*. San Francisco: City Lights Books, 1996.

Gordon, Avery and Christopher Newfield, eds. *Mapping Multiculturalism*. Minnesota: University of Minnesota Press, 1996.

Government of Canada. *A Report of the Canadian Immigration and Population Study: Immigration Policy Perspective*. Ottawa: Department of Manpower and Immigration and Information Canada, 1974.

———. *Royal Commission Report on Equality in Employment*. Ottawa: Ministry of Supply and Services, 1984.

———. *Equality Now: Report of the Special Committee on Visible Minorities*. Ottawa: House of Commons, 1986.

Gramsci, Antonio. "State and Civil Society." In Quentin Hoare and Geoffrey Smith, eds. and trans. *Selections from the Prison Notebooks*, 210-276. New York: International Publishers, 1971.

Hall, Stuart. "New Ethnicities." In James Donald and Ali Ratansi, eds. 'Race', Culture and Difference, 252-260. London: Sage, 1992.

Hamilton, Roberta, ed. The Politics of Diversity. Boston: Beacon Press, 1986.

Hobsbawm, Eric and Terence Ranger, eds. The Invention of Tradition. Cambridge: Cambridge University Press, 1984.

Ismail, Qadri and Pradeep Jeganathan, eds. Unmaking the Nation: The Politics of Identity and History in Modern Sri Lanka. Colombo: Social Scientists' Association, 1995.

Kulchyski, Peter, ed. Unjust Relations: Aboriginal Rights in Canadian Courts. Toronto: University of Toronto Press, 1994.

Kymlicka, Will. Multicultural Citizenship: A Liberal Theory of Minority Rights. Oxford: Clarendon Press, 1995.

Law Union of Ontario. The Immigrants Handbook. Montreal: Black Rose Books, 1981.

Li, Peter S. "Chinese Investment and Business in Canada: Ethnic Entrepreneurship Reconsidered." Pacific Affairs 66, no. 2 (1993), 219-243.

Mani, Lata. "Contentious Traditions: The Debate on Sati in Colonial India." In Kumkum Sangari and Sudesh Vaid, eds. Recasting Women: Essays in Indian Colonial History, 88-126. New Brunswick, New Jersey: Rutgers University Press, 1989.

McLaren, Peter, ed. Revolutionary Multiculturalism: Pedagogies of Dissent in the New Millennium. Boulder, Colorado: Westview Press, 1997.

McPherson, C. B. The Life and Times of Liberal Democracy. Oxford: Oxford University Press, 1977.

Modood, Tariq. "Political Blackness and British Asians." Sociology 28, no. 3 (1990), 859-876.

Mohanty, Chandra, Ann Russo, and Lourdes Torres, eds. Third World Women and the Politics of Feminism. Bloomington, Indiana: Indiana University Press, 1991.

Monture-Angus, Patricia. Thunder in My Soul: A Mohawk Woman Speaks. Halifax, Nova Scotia: Fernwood Press, 1995.

Ng, Roxana. "Sexism, Racism, Canadian Nationalism." In Himani Bannerji, ed. Returning the Gaze: Essays on Racism, Feminism and Politics, 223-241. Toronto: Sister Vision Press, 1993.

Parenti, Michael. Dirty Truths. San Francisco: City Lights Books, 1996.

Parmar, Pratibha. "Black Feminism: The Politics of Articulation." In Jonathan Rutherford, ed. Identity, Community, Culture, Difference, 101-126. London: Lawrence and Wishart, 1990.

Porter, John. The Vertical Mosaic. Toronto: University of Toronto Press, 1965.

Radcliffe-Brown, Alfred R. *Structure and Function in Primitive Society*. New York: The Free Press, 1965.

Robinson, Cedric. "Manichaeism and Multiculturalism." In Avery Gordon and Christopher Newfield, eds. *Mapping Multiculturalism*, 116-124. Minneapolis, Minnesota: University of Minnesota Press, 1996.

Roman, Leslie. "White is a Color! White Defensiveness, Postmodernism and Anti-Racist Pedagogy." In Warren Crichlow and Cameron McCarthy, eds. *Race, Identity and Representation in Education*, 71-88. New York and London: Routledge, 1993.

Sandoval, Chela. "U.S. Third World Feminism: The Theory and Method of Oppositional Consciousness in the Postmodern World." *Genders* 10 (1991), 1-24.

Shivanandan. *A Different Hunger: Writings on Black Resistance*. London: Pluto Press, 1982.

Skeldon, Ronald, ed. *Emigration from Hong Kong: Tendencies and Impacts*. Hong Kong: Chinese University Press, 1995.

Smith, Dorothy E. *The Conceptual Practices of Power: A Feminist Sociology of Knowledge*. Toronto: University of Toronto Press, 1990.

Spelman, Elizabeth. *Inessential Woman: Problems of Exclusion in Feminist Thought*. Boston: Beacon Press, 1988.

Stoler, Ann Laura. *Race and the Education of Desire*. Durham, N.C. and London: Duke University Press, 1995.

Sudbury, Julia. *'Other Kinds of Dreams': Black Women's Organizations and the Politics of Transformation*. London and New York: Routledge, 1998.

Taylor, Charles. *Multiculturalism and 'the Politics of Recognition.'* Princeton: Princeton University Press, 1992.

———. *Reconciling the Solitudes: Essays on Canadian Federalism and Nationalism*. Montreal: McGill-Queen's University Press, 1993.

Trudeau, Pierre. *Federalism and the French Canadians*, trans. Patricia Claxton. Toronto: MacMillan, 1968.

Volpp, Leti. "Misidentifying Culture: Asian Women and the Cultural Defense." *Harvard Women's Law Journal* 17 (1994), 57-101.

Wallace, Michelle. "The Search for the 'Good Enough' Mammy: Multiculturalism, Popular Culture and Psychoanalysis." In Theo Goldberg, ed. *Multiculturalism: A Critical Reader*, 259-268. Oxford: Blackwell, 1994.

Williams, Raymond. *Problems in Materialism and Culture*. London: Verso, 1980.

Wong, Lloyd. "Globalization and Transnational Migration: A Study of Recent Chinese Capitalist Migration from the Asian Pacific to Canada." *International Sociology* 12, no. 3 (1997), 329-351.

CHAPTER 2

Geography Lessons:
On Being an Insider/Outsider
to the Canadian Nation

*M*y first encounter with Canada occurred during my geography lessons as a young girl. There, in an atlas of physical geography, coloured green, pink, and yellow, I came across Canada — a place of trees, lakes, wheat fields, ice caps, and an ancient rock formation cut through with glaciers. I don't remember reading anything of the history of this country in my geography book, but somehow there were faint echoes of people and nature blurring into each other — "red Indians," "eskimos," "igloos," "aurora borealis," and "reindeer." From where did these images come if not from my geography book? From literature and scattered visual images perhaps? There were, after all, the books of Fenimore Cooper or Jack London, which irrespective of national boundaries created mythologies of the "North," the "Indian," and wove tales of discovery of the Arctic — of Amundsen and others lost in blizzards on their dog sleds. Eventually, on my fourteenth birthday, I received a book called *The Scalpel and the Sword*, and I decided to be a doctor, like Norman Bethune.

What I am trying to recount is what Canada meant for me — all this jumbled-up information, this fusion of people and nature, my imagination moved by forests and the glow of Arctic ice. Certainly, "Canada" was a mental rather than a historical space. It was an idyllic construction of nature and adventure.

Many years later, the Canada I stepped into was vastly different from the Canada I had constructed in my childhood. When I immigrated to Montreal, I stepped out of my romantic construction of Canada and into a distinctly political-ideological one — one which impressed me as being both negative and aggressive. From the insistence and harshness with which I was asked whether I intended to apply for "landing" — a term I did not understand and that had to be explained — I knew that I was not welcome in this "Canada." I told the officer defiantly that this would never be my country; I had come as a foreign student and would leave upon receiving my degree. That is how it has remained to this day. Had I been received differently, had I been made to feel more "at home," would this be my home, my Canada?

This remains a hypothetical question, since upon "landing" six years later and being labelled an "immigrant," a "visible minority woman," I have remained in limbo. Even after years of being an "immigrant," and upon swearing allegiance to the same Queen of England from whom India had parted, I was not to be a "Canadian." Regardless of my official status as a Canadian citizen, I, like many others, remained an "immigrant." The category "Canadian" clearly applied to people who had two things in common: their white skin and their European North American (not Mexican) background. They did not all speak English. There were two colors in this political atlas — one a beige-brown shading off into black and the other white. These shades did not simply reflect skin colors — they reflected the ideological, political, and cultural assumptions and administrative practices of the Canadian State.

"Canada" then cannot be taken as a given. It is obviously a construction, a set of representations, embodying certain types of political and cultural communities and their operations. These communities were themselves constructed in agreement with certain ideas regarding skin color, history, language (English/French), and other cultural signifiers — all of which may be subsumed under the ideological category "white."[1] A "Canada" constructed on this basis contains certain notions of nation, state formation, and economy. Europeanness as "whiteness"[2] thus translates into "Canada" and provides it with its "imagined community." This is a process that Benedict Anderson (1991) speaks of, but he glosses over the divisiveness of class, "race," and ideology — the irreconcilable contradictions at the heart of this community-nation-state project. Furthermore, he does not ask about the type of imagination at work in this project. He does not ask either *whose* imagination is advanced as the national imaginary or what this has to do with organizing practical and ideological exclusions and inclusions within the national space. These questions become concrete if we look at how I was received in Canada. Why was I thus received? Was it just an accident? An isolated instance? What did it have to do with *who* I was — my so-called gender and race? Did this story of mine begin with my arrival, or was I just a tiny episode in a pre-existing historical narrative? Can I or similar "others" imagine a "Canada" and project it as the national imaginary?

So if we problematize the notion of "Canada" through the introjection of the idea of belonging, we are left with the paradox of both belonging and non-belonging simultaneously. As a population, we non-whites and women (in particular, non-white women) are living in a specific territory. We are part of its economy, subject to its laws, and members of its civil society. Yet we are not part of its self-definition as "Canada" because we are not "Canadians." We are pasted over with labels that give us identities that are extraneous to us. And these labels originate in the ideology of the nation, in the Canadian state apparatus, in the media, in the education system, and in the commonsense world of common parlance. We ourselves use them. They are familiar, naturalized names: visible minorities, immigrants, newcomers, refugees, aliens, illegals, people of color, multicultural communities, and so on. We are sexed into immigrant women, women of colour, visible minority women, black/South Asian/Chinese women, ESL (English as second language) speakers, and many more.[3] The names keep proliferating, as though there were a seething reality, unmanageable and uncontainable in any one name. Concomitant with this mania for the naming of "others" is one for the naming of that which is "Canadian." This "Canadian" core community is defined through the same process that others us. We, with our named and ascribed otherness, face an undifferentiated notion of the "Canadian" as the unwavering beacon of our assimilation.

And what is the function of the many names applied to us? They are categories for organizing the state apparatus, its regulations and policy functions, and for enabling the ideological organization of "relations of ruling."[4] These categories enable the state to extend its governing and administrative jurisdiction into civil society, while, at the same time, incorporating the everyday person into the national project. One might say, then, remembering Althusser, that they are appellations for interpellation.[5] These names are codes for political subjectivities and ideological/pedagogical possibilities, and they have embedded in them both immediate and long-term political effects. They help to construct "Canada" and to place us in certain roles and niches of the nation; and those who are not "Canadians" cannot directly project "Canada." This "Canada's" placement of "others," because it creates feelings of belonging and alienation, not only produces psychological and cultural problems regarding power, but is also integral to the structure of the Canadian polity itself. Its categories of otherness delimit the membership of this nation and this state (Ng, 1993). This situation reveals not only a raced or ethnicized state, but also — more importantly — a crisis in citizenship and a continual attempt to manage this crisis. It tells us that, in the polity of Canadian liberal democracy, there is always already a crisis of gender, race, and class. This becomes obvious if we look at the status of women, in particular the status of white women, in terms of their participation in the construction of "Canada." Their protracted struggle for enfranchisement, for inclusion in the nation, is marked by the fact that their gender was a barrier to them in spite of their status as mothers and daughters of the Canadian white male "race." Although Canadian suffragists such as Nellie McClung, following their white U.S. sisters, resented Chinese and non-white enfranchisement, they themselves were considered to be second-class citizens.[6] Privileged by class and race, but handicapped by gender, their situation exposes the fact that citizenship does not provide automatic membership in the nation's community. Living in a nation does not, by definition, provide one with a prerogative to "imagine" it. From the very inception of democracy, Athenian and after, the making of a national imaginary, the construction of its ideological political form and content, has been conditional. Such privilege, manifested as a belonging and conforming to regulatory norms and forms, has been restricted through criteria that are both constructed through and anchored in the social relations of the civil society. Being working class, being "raced," and being of a certain gender, all restrict access to citizenship in the here and now by modifying the conditions of freedom, property, and literacy.

Under circumstances in which wives and daughters of the white bourgeoisie do not qualify for citizenship, the issue of the enfranchisement of non-white women (usually working class) becomes ever more problematic. The latter are virtually erased from the political map. The non-white working-class male is at least referred to in the course of white bourgeois women's drives for social agency and citizenship, but their female counterparts are not even mentioned as potential members.[7] The othering or difference that is produced through the state's racist or ethnicizing policies with regard to importing and administrating labour[8] could only be further intensified through gendering. General disenfranchisement, deportation, head taxes, barrack lives, and so on (followed in more recent times by various types of immigration and refugee statuses, the reintroduction of a form of head tax through application fees, etc.) gave momentum to further oppression through patriarchy. Together, "sexing" and "racing" mark moments in a probation which qualifies one for a merely *formal equality* a nominal citizenship.[9]

The making of Canada is thus accomplished through the exclusion and marginalization of women. Even formal equality has been hard for women to come by. Although not explicitly stated in the Constitution, this exclusive gendering is clearly present in the case of imported labour. At lower levels of labour, particularly, there was (and is) an active attempt to seek able-bodied young men in the industrial/manufacturing sector and young women in the service sector or for industrial piece-work.[10] This, too, was racialized and ethnicized as white and non-white, with the former being given permission to create families, to "settle" Canada and outnumber its indigenous peoples, and the latter, Chinese and Indian indentured workers, being restricted through head taxes, quotas, and miscegenation laws. A non-white labourer lived in a state of continual vulnerability, driven underground in search of jobs, company, and sex.[11] Even in the 1950s, when emigrating from the

Third World with families first became possible, the emphasis was on masculinizing the labor force. "Independent immigration," therefore, has been a male preserve, with most women entering Canada "sponsored" by, or as "dependents" of, the "head of a family." This is the case even when women are as skilled (or unskilled) as their husbands. This patriarchal gesture of the state gave women's husbands (or male sponsors) complete control over them, while domestic workers (also, for the most part, women) were in the grip of their "Canadian" employers. Battering, rape, and general degradation could not and cannot be effectively resisted without risking the breakdown of these sponsorships, the withdrawal of work permits, and deportation. So, not only is there a mandate for importing able-bodied adult male labour and female reproducers (whose social production costs have been borne by another country), there is also a continual attempt to patriarchalize Canada's social organization. Thus, in Canada, gender and race have always mediated the overall social production and relations of class.

This patriarchalization has been at work since the era of the fur trade. It intensified when the white settler colonial state emerged, having race and gender deeply engraved in both its definition and its administration.[12] The socio-economic and cultural disenfranchisement of indigenous peoples has been both genocidal and patriarchal. Through the Indian Act, for example, racist and sexist constructions of "the Indian," "Indian culture," and "the Indian woman" became both possible and practicable.[13] This went together with ensuring that the white woman was out of bounds for non-white men, a process that did not exhaust itself with old-style settler colonialism. Canadian social organization was based on race, which was defined as being constituted by those of "pure blood" (either "Indians" or "Europeans") and those of "mixed blood" (the Métis).[14] The Indian Act created a zone of non-identity for indigenous women, and it ensured that they lost their economic bases. By marrying out of their prescribed locations and blood spaces as "Indians," they lost their "Indian" status in their own communities and did not gain white status in the non-Native communities.[15] This was a part of the overall process of excluding women from "Canada," and it came down most heavily on "raced" others.

In more recent times, the organized subordination of women comes out clearly in the context of the pro-choice movement, which is led by middle-class white women. Given that we live in a so-called liberal democracy (which supposedly enshrines individual rights and freedom of choice), and given that we live in what C. B. Macpherson has called a "market model of democracy" (Macpherson, 1977; 1973, 157-203), there should be no proscription against obtaining abortion on demand. But in spite of their formal equality with men as "citizens" and their being defined as possessive individuals, as owners of their own persons and other property, women's rights to abortion on demand is opposed by the Canadian state. And, their white, middle-class status notwithstanding, the leaders of the pro-choice movement were revealed to be, in political-ideological terms, of minority or non-age status. Unlike a man, who could consent to surgical procedures on any part of his body, a woman was against a legal wall. In fact, women turned out to be wards of the state, which, as their paternal guardian, got to decide what was good for them. With the help of protective/preventive laws and masculinized expert medical services, women were held in permanent tutelage. This role of reluctant breeders is forced, particularly, on white women, as they are of the majority culture and are thus held responsible for counterbalancing the "unassimilables" (i.e., non-whites) among us. Besides, as non-white women are considered to be overly fecund, there is a terror that they might change Canada's racial composition. Bloc Québecois leader Lucien Bouchard, while on his separatist campaign, has put the responsibility of the success of his national project squarely in the lap of Quebec's white women, since it is they who must breed in order to prop up the declining "white race."[16] In various euphemistic forms, this argument has underpinned Canadian immigration, refugee, and cultural policies. It is not hard to see that the Canadian state's overwhelming sense of guardianship over women's bodies amounts to a demand for white women to reproduce more and for non-white women to reproduce less. The overall mandate for women, here as in China (which has become a byword for repressive reproductive regimes), is to reproduce in keeping with the economic, cultural, and political ambitions of the state and within an overall population policy projected for the country. In the end, nationally appropriate reproduction becomes the white woman's burden, and it is not coincidental that this dovetails with the white supremacist desire to "Keep Canada White."

The fact that the state seeks to hold the white woman's womb hostage has profound repercussions for non-white women. Caught in the same legal labyrinth as are their white counterparts, their motherhood is by implication also regulated. In the United States, a vast number of black women do not reach natural menopause (Sheehy, 1991); they are given complete hysterectomies or tubal ligations as early as during their thirties. It would be interesting to do a comparative study of the difficulties faced by black and white women, respectively, in their attempts to obtain abortions in Canada; it would also be interesting to look at this research in terms of class. At this point, however, I can only point to the general discouragement meted out to non-white people with regard to reproduction. Since there is already an attempt to criminalize "immigrants" or "visible minorities," any non-white woman's violation of the state's mandate against abortion on demand threatens to further criminalize her.

The issue of "motherhood" should lead us to think about the status of women in Canada in general, and about women's location in the racialized and gendered political economy. It is interesting that when even minimum cognizance is taken of the exclusion of women, the state (e.g., Mike Harris's Ontario) rushes in to smash whatever ineffectual equity programs may have been put in place due to pressure from the women's movement. On the other hand, the state continues, in the language of christian charity, to demonize women as recipients of social welfare.

The state constructs not only women in general, but also poor women, and impoverished women of color in particular, as political/ social subjects who are essentially dependent and weak (Fraser and Gordon, 1994; Alexander and Mohanty, 1997). As such they are seen as a burden on the state and the economy; that is, on the more competent, economically productive, masculinized "tax payer." The welfare recipient is often portrayed as a "she" — a "welfare mother"

or a "single mother." Thanks to the combined effort of the state
and the media, poverty is "feminized." It is seen as located in
women's own social subjectivity, as their own creation. A whole
world is conjured up — a world of mothers, strollers, babies, and
recalcitrant, badly brought up children. This "female culture of
poverty" is then condemned by the school system, child
psychologists, the Ministry of Social Services, and the Ministry of
Correctional Services. In fact, we are currently witnessing the revival
of an eighteenth- and nineteenth-century category known as "the
poor." "The poor" are now emerging as a character type, as (almost)
a separate species. As with women, so with the poor in general:
their character is their destiny. Not only does this category hide
the production of poverty by the state and the ruling mores of
capital, it also results in a kind of political paralysis through the
ontologization of poverty. The only action taken on behalf of the
poor has to do with charity and the reinforcement of the nuclear
family — action that assuages the consciences of the charitable rather
than the hunger of those in need. It is worth considering what a
very different political and social persona would be projected if,
rather than being categorized as "the poor," this same group of
people was categorized as "the proletariat."

Racialization affects "the poor" just as it does others, such as
unemployed workers. The category "immigrant/refugee welfare
recipient," for example, includes both men and women who are
thoroughly demonized as perennial welfare recipients and
manipulators of unemployment insurance and workers' disability
pension. The odour of dishonesty that haunts the world of "the
poor" in general is most intense around those who are non-white.
Whole communities live under suspicion and surveillance —
Somalis, Tamils, Jamaicans, and so on. This raced poverty is both
masculine and feminine, and even its feminine face does not fall
within any code of chivalry or compassion and charity. Because of
the alleged illegitimacy of their presence in Canada, these people
are not candidates for such treatment. This segment of "the poor"
is thus quickly covered in a mantle of crime. The world of non-
white poverty inspires media/state-produced images of desperate
young men always ready to commit crime. What is aimed at them
is "order" — either that of the police officer's gun or that of the

deportation law. Both poor non-white men and non-white women are under permanent suspicion of "welfare fraud," a heightened version of what confronts poor whites.

That my assertions are not a matter of individual paranoia is evident in the fact that Ontario has established a "hotline" to prompt us to report anonymously on our neighbours and anyone else whom we think might be cheating "the system." This "snitch line" violates human dignity/human rights, creates a state of legal surveillance, and organizes people into vigilante-style relationships with one another. It brings racism and sexism to a boiling point by stimulating an everyday culture of racist sexism, and it creates an atmosphere that can only be described as fascistic. Clearly, reporting "the jew" among us is not over yet!

Since these race-gendered class forms of criminalization, marginalization, and exclusion arise in present-day Canada — a supposedly liberal democratic state — the situation with which we have to deal becomes highly complex. Canada is not talked about in the same way as is, for example, South Africa. Its "Indian" reserves are not seen as Bantustans (the latter were apparently inspired by the former).[17] Canada as a liberal democracy cannot, in spite of the Reform Party or the police view of non-white communities, practice legal apartheid. The Canadian state, according to its Charter of Rights and Freedoms, claims not to discriminate on the bases of race, gender, and so on. But it is obvious that, by its very organization of social communities in "race" and ethnic terms, the state constantly creates "Canadians" and "others." This happens not only in the realm of state constructed policy, but also in that of everyday life — within what Theo Goldberg (1993) calls a "racist culture." This "racist culture" is in a mutually constitutive relationship with the state.

If we do not accept this, then the racist violence of the Canadian Airborne Regiment in Somalia in the course of its peace-keeping duties for the United Nations becomes an instance of insanity. But if we see racism as a hegemonic social and political culture and practice participated in by the police, the military, the other aspects of the state, the church, the educational system, and our everyday life, then what happened in Somalia begins to make some sociological sense. This pervasive "racist culture," which is textured through and through with the cult of "raced" masculinity, cannot but claim its victims. To be a "white man," then, is not a simple physical fact; it is a moral imperative and an ideology.[18] Sometimes it works in a crude manner, as in white supremacist groups; sometimes it is more refined, as in the languages of civilization and expertise. But it is not all that far from Canadian engineering students' sexist-racist rites to the Airborne's hazing and killing in Somalia. Canada's fundamentally patriarchal character is evident from Somalia to Oka, from Gustafson Lake to Ipperwash,[19] and in the police shooting of black youths, including that of Sophia Cook,[20] and the street-corner strip-search of another woman, Audrey Smith.[21] Canada's racist patriarchal nature is further exemplified by the fact that it is so often culturally represented abroad by the Royal Canadian Mounted Police on postcards manufactured for tourist consumption. A secret police that is publicly advertised as "Canadian culture" — quite a plug for white masculinity.

In the face of my assertion that "Canada," as a national imaginary, is a sexist-racist entity, some will advance a phenomenon known as "multiculturalism."[22] I will be told that, due to this phenomenon, which needs especial scrutiny with regard to citizenship of "others," the whole world looks up to Canada. Although, in practice, multiculturalism has never been effective, it can and does serve as an ideological slogan within a liberal democratic framework. It supplies an administrative device for managing social contradictions and conflicts. This is important since "Canada," as a nationalist project, is perceived to be a homogeneous, solid, and settled entity, though its history constantly belies this.

This is why the language for imagining "Canada" is fraught with such notions as "solitude" and "survival." There is in this national space a legitimation crisis.[23] Other than the dissent and struggle of the indigenous peoples, the raced-gendered "others" who remain a source of dissentience, the national project is deeply riven by the rivalry between anglophones and francophones — Canada's "two solitudes."[24] Equally patriarchal and race inscribed, these two solitudes remain central cultural/political actors, covering over the seething "Indian question," which continually erupts in the form of land claims and demands for self-determination and self-government.[25] A creation of violent and illegal settlers (to whom no one had issued "landing" permits), "Canada" remains an unformed union, its particularist and partisan state formation frequently showing through. Yet a state cannot become liberal and democratic without an element of transcendence.[26] And what, after all, could give Canada the appearance of transcendence as well as "multiculturalism," with its slogan "unity in diversity"? The drive for making an anglo-North American Canada is partly assuaged by this ideological gesture. "Immigrants " especially "visible minorities," become useful with regard to challenging the substantive claim of more well-entrenched "others" (i.e., the Québecois or indigenous peoples), who cannot be deported to their "home" countries. Nominally and opportunistically introducing those others as entities in the national imaginary, the notion/nation of "Canada" attempts to overcome its legitimation crisis. It is in this way that every social and economic demand can be gutted and reduced to the level of the cultural/symbolic. Ironically, immigrant "others," who serve as categories of exclusion in Canada's nation-making ideology, become an instrument for creating a sphere of transcendence. The state claims to rise above all partisan interests and functions as an arbitrator between different cultural groups. This is the moral high ground, the political instrument with which the state maintains the hegemony of an anglo-Canada. We might say that it is these oppressed "others" who gave Canada the gift of multiculturalism. In any case, armed with the ideological tool of multiculturalism, Canada manages its crisis in legitimation and citizenship. It offers the Québecois and the First Nations peoples a part in the "national unity," albeit an empty one, while denying them their own governments as separatist enterprises.

Fractured by race, gender, class, and long-standing colonial rivalries, the construction of "Canada" entails two major forms of interconnected crises — that of citizenship and that of the legitimation of a "national" state formation. Differential status in citizenship is paired with a dual state formation, each aspect of which exerts pressures on the other. A white settler colonial state and a liberal democracy, while historically and contingently connected in many cases (such as in Australia, the former South Africa, the United States, the former Rhodesia [Zimbabwe], or Canada) are two separate political projects. They are not genealogically connected in terms of their political ideals and governing structures. This becomes clearer when we look at Britain, which had a vast colonial empire and ruled it autocratically, while developing a liberal democracy inside the country. In liberal democracy, even if it is only in the sphere of polity, the same state structures and legalities govern the entire subject population and show a reliance on the notion of enlightenment. The liberal democratic state, at least at the level of *formal equality*, is the antithesis of a colonial state. But in Canada, as in the case of Australia, for example, certain features of the colonial state coexist with those of a liberal democracy (Watkins, 1977). Different laws, with special departments such as the Department of Indian Affairs in Canada, govern the population differently. Indian reserves have laws governing them economically, politically, and socially which are different from the laws governing the rest of Canada. Viewed from the standpoint of indigenous peoples, the state of Canada is based on class, gender, and race, and it continues to administer these reserves as would a colonial state. Even the territorial question is still unsettled, while containment strategies typical of colonial states continue to be in evidence around the administration of reserves. These colonial relations manifest themselves in conflicts around the James Bay Project, Oka, Gustafson Lake, Ipperwash, and so on. Debates on Native self-determination or First Nations self-government further reveal the colonial relations between Canada and its indigenous peoples. According to some scholars, Canada's dual state formation (a liberal democracy with a colonial heart) is matched by a dual economy. Theories of world system and dependency, usually applied to ex-colonized countries, are considered to be applicable to Canada.[27] It is claimed that there is a metropole-peripheral economy within, while the country as a whole displays features of advanced industrial capitalism along with its dependency on foreign, especially U.S., capital.[28] This convoluted state of affairs has given rise to peculiar social formations, whereby colonized nations continue to exist within the "Canadian" nation state. Acknowledged as the First Nations, Native peoples are like the Palestinians, who form a nation without a state and are subject to continual repression. The role that "race" has played in the context of colonization is obvious. Subsequently a dependent but imperialist capital has continued to organize an economy and a society based on "race." It is not surprising that talk of cultural identities in this country quickly veers toward racialization. Not only is "the Indian," so called, a category of "race," but so are other cultural categories used for non-white immigrants tinged with "race."

These colonial relations and representations of "Canada," which run like rich veins throughout its state formation, were overlayered with liberal democratic aspirations in the course of the latter half of the twentieth century. The state faced many contradictions and complexities in this project due to the persistence of the colonial relations and also to the country's own inability to have a bourgeois revolution. Lacking a fully articulated bourgeois class in leadership Canada has in effect a double dependency — on Britain for governmental and certain cultural forms, and on the U.S. for capital as well as for social and political culture.[29] Like all liberal democracies it is not only capitalist, but, as I said, colonial and dependent and autonomously imperialist at the same time. The problems of coherent state formation multiply as a result.

In fact, in the face of Canada's settler colonial origin and the weak development of its capital and capitalist class, the state in Canada has been a direct agent for capitalist development and has performed a substantial role in the accumulation of capital. It has also been the chief agent for procuring labour and creating a labour market, and has assisted in the regulation and exploitation of labour. Canada has depended on imported labour and has organized the labour market along lines of "race" and gender. This was not often an activity undertaken by the accumulating classes but primarily performed by the state, which took over a vast portion of the role of facilitation.[30] The current obedience of the state to NAFTA, or corporate transnational capital, is highly symptomatic of this. "Race" or ethnicity, translated into immigration policy quotas, has actually located different types of labour in different productional recesses.

By locking immigrant workers into zones of menial labour and low wages, the state has brought down the wage structure of the country as a whole. It has actively de-skilled and marginalized Third World immigrants by decertifying them and forcing them into the working class. Long before the present economic crisis, this device had created a reserve army of labour consisting of both males and females. As any study of homeworkers, piece-workers, cleaners of public spaces, or domestics will show, non-white or "immigrant" women occupy the worst position among these marginalized labour groups (Johnson and Johnson, 1982). These, then, are the people — straddling the line between surplus exploitation and unemployment — who stand permanently on the threshold of Canadian citizenship. Their paper-thin status is revealed when some family members are deported while others, such as children born in Canada, are allowed to stay. If these are not sufficient reminders of the crises of citizenship faced by non-white "others," one need only remember the Japanese internment.[31]

This situation is guaranteed to produce a double crisis of legitimation, one for the state and one for its citizens. The heart of the matter lies in the fact that a colonial, partisan anglo-Canada has arrogated to itself the task of constructing "Canada" while being economically dependent on foreign investment capital. This anglo-Canada has neither moral high ground nor economic solvency to justify its hegemony. The notions of "Canada" and "Canadian" are mocked by gigantic question marks.

During the course of its tortuous formation, Canada has continued exude irreconcilable contradictions. In following the imperatives of liberal democracy, in being motivated by the ideal of pluralism, and in responding to popular protests against inequality, Canada promulgated both multiculturalism and affirmative action, which both contained dissatisfaction and legitimated existing inequalities. At the same time, through various debates, the state called for sexist and racist responses to all its so-called multiculturalist and equity-oriented proposals. For example, at this moment, the fig leaf of equity and affirmative action has been altogether dropped in Ontario. By constantly calling on and constructing an entity called "Canadians" and pitting it against immigrants, the state has actually stimulated white supremacist attitudes and helped to establish their organizations, as was revealed by a government agent with regard to the Heritage Front.[32] By constantly signifying the white population as "Canadians" and immigrants of color as "others," by constantly stereotyping Third World immigrants as criminals, terrorists, and fundamentalists, the state manages to both manipulate and cancel its alleged dedication to multiculturalism.

A most dangerous state use of racism occurs with regard to its own socio-economic failures and its inability to cope with the violence inherent within structural adjustment. Since the state and the media jointly portray immigrants from non-white, poor countries as "the problem," it is not surprising that the white population looks at them as the villains of the piece — as "those people who took away our jobs." These immigrants, in turn, look among themselves to find someone to blame for the economic and social disaster they face. Interestingly, this attitude does not apply to eastern Europeans, who are poor but white.

Due to its selective modes of ethnicization, multiculturalism is itself a vehicle for racialization. It establishes anglo-Canadian culture as the ethnic core culture while "tolerating" and hierarchically arranging others around it as "multiculture." The ethics and aesthetics of "whiteness," with its colonial imperialist/racist ranking criteria, define and construct the "multi" culture of Canada's others. This reified, mutated product, accomplished through a web of hierarchically arranged stereotypes, can then be both used against "ethnic" communities and commoditized with regard to fashion and current market tastes. Festivals of "ethnic" communities, from the Toronto Caravan to Caribana, provide excellent examples. Such "ethnic" constructs have serious consequences in the perpetuation of violence against women. Frequently, in the name of cultural sensitivity and respect, the state does not address violence against women when it occurs among the multiculturally defined "ethnic" communities. It is rumoured that the accused's behavior is a part of "their culture," and that "they" are traditional, fundamentalist, and uncivilized. In this way, an entire population is demonized even though particular men become exempt from indictment. Similarly, Canada's islamic population has become permanently associated with terrorism and every Arab is seen as a potential terrorist.

One more issue that needs to be stressed with regard to multiculturalism is the fact that it arises at the convergence of a struggle between the state and otherized, especially non-white, subjects. Their demands for justice, for effective anti-racist policies and administration, for the right to a substantive social and cultural life, are overdetermined by the agenda of the state. As long as "multiculturalism" only skims the surface of society, expressing itself as traditional ethics, such as arranged marriages, and ethnic food, clothes, songs and dances (thus facilitating tourism), it is tolerated by the state and "Canadians" as non-threatening. But if the demands go a little deeper than that (e.g., teaching "other" religions or languages), they produce violent reaction, indicating a deep resentment toward funding "others'" arts and cultures. This can be seen in the Reform Party's stance on immigration and multiculturalism.

The convergence of gender and race oppression in Canada became explicit in the reactions to the New Democratic Party's (NDP) proposal for affirmative action. It was a proposal that extended inclusivity to Canada's women, visible minorities, aboriginal people, francophones, and disabled people. The reaction was severe, and it reverberated throughout the entire country — professors and truck drivers displaying the same response. National newspapers advertised the proposal as "whites need not apply" or "white males need not apply." This is a curious reading, since it completely overlooks the fact that the legislation is in keeping with liberal pluralism, which entails minimal representation. The violent responses also made one realize that the ideologies of race and gender, respectively, are connected. If white women, disabled people, and francophones are not to be recognized as white, we are left to ask: "What is whiteness?" The issue of gender is also revealing. If francophones and disabled people, no matter what their colour, are not to be recognized as "males," then what is masculinity? Does speaking French exclude people from being "white males"?

This instance serves to show that "Canada," as a national imaginary, its multiculturalism and its lip service to Quebec's Canadianness notwithstanding, is actually an anglo-white male idea that blurs the class lines. There is little in the state's notion of multiculturalism that speaks to social justice. More than anything else, multiculturalism preserves the partisan nature of the state by helping to contain pressures exerted by "others" for social justice and equity.

We might, at this point, be asked what legitimized Canada, what provided the basis for its national project, before the arrival of the concept of multiculturalism. What was its justificatory, politically existential discourse? It seems that it was the notion of "survival."[31] The white settler colonial entity devised for itself a threatened identity, whereby the colonizer (erasing colonialism) was faced with the danger of extinction. In the works of Margaret Atwood (1972b), such a state of affairs is advanced as a truism, as a fact of "Canada." In Atwood's novel *Surfacing* (1972a), for example, a woman discovers her violated- and invaded-self in, or as, an equally violated and invaded wilderness. In spite of her gender and feminism, her race and class allow Atwood to project this particular vision of Canada. But this metaphor of the political psyche of Canada as a threatened femininity/nature obliterates indigenous people, swallowing them up in the myth of an empty wilderness that is to be invaded and populated by white people. In doing this, Atwood follows a literary and artistic tradition already in place, for example, in many of the works of the Group of Seven (Watson, 1994). The "Canadian," as the dreamer of the nation, must come to terms with the wilderness in order to find and found "Canada." S/he is white/European. The indigenous peoples are either not there or are one with the primal, non-human forces of nature. The threat to Canada, then, comes not only from south of its border but from within itself — from its denied, unincorporated, alienated nature and its human forms. In reaction to this can the settler, "the Canadian," take an option that Atwood's heroine in *Surfacing*, being a "woman" and pacifist, cannot? Can he, as he is a man, feel justified in killing or conquering that which he cannot comprehend or finally conquer? The "survival" ideological space holds that possibility in suspense. The other threat to Canada comes from without — from its fear of being overrun by, and incorporated into, the United States. This formulation, while anti-American and mildly anti-imperialist, erases Canada's own colonial and imperialist nature and aspirations. And this erasure certainly does not help to create politics or policies that challenge anglo-white nationalism, with its masculinist inflection, and that call for other ways of imagining and administering Canada.

The possibilities for constructing a radically different Canada emerge only from those who have been "othered" as the insider-outsiders of the nation. It is their standpoints which, oppositionally politicized, can take us beyond the confines of gender and race and enable us to challenge class through a critical and liberating vision. In their lives, politics, and work, the "others" hold the possibility of being able to expose the hollowness of the liberal state and to provide us with an understanding of both the refined and crude constructions of "white power" behind "Canada's" national imaginary. They serve to remind us of the Canada that *could* exist.

NOTES

1   On the construction of "whiteness" as an ideological, political, and socio-historical category, see Allen (1994), Frankenberg (1993), Roediger (1993), Roman (1993), and Ware (1991).

2   On Europeanness as "whiteness," see Stoller (1995).

3   See Carty and Brand (1993) and Carty (1994).

4   See D. E. Smith (1987), 3 ,5-6, for a definition of this term.

5   For Althusser's concept of interpellation, see Althusser (1971,162-70).

6   Much has been written on the suffrage struggle and second-class citizen status of white bourgeois women. For particular connections between these themes and the issue of race, see Stoller (1995) and Davis (1983).

7   See hooks (1981), chapters 4 and 5; Collins (1990), chapter 4; and B. Smith (1982).

8   On how the Canadian labour market and class system is organized through race and ethnicity, see Bolaria and Li (1988) and Avery (1995).

9   Much work still needs to be done with regard to considering class formation in terms of both race and gender, but Brand (1991) makes a beginning. See also Brand and Bhaggiyadatta (1985).

10   This is powerfully brought forth in the issue of the importation of domestic workers to Toronto from the Caribbean. See Silvera (1989).

11   See Bolaria and Li (1988), chapters 5, 7, and 8; and Arnopoulos (1979).

12   On Canada as a white settler colony and race/gender inscriptions in the formation and workings of the state, see Kulchyski (1994), Tester and Kulchyski (1994), and Monture-Angus (1995).

13   See Francis (1992). Also, Monture-Angus (1995) says: "The definition of Indian is a legal one based on the necessity of identifying the population against which

bureaucrats will administer the *Indian Act* regime. This definition is based on blood lines and residency on a reserve" (122, n. 5).

14 See Campbell (1983) and Emberley (1993).

15 See chapter 5 in Kulchyski (1994).

16 This was part of Lucien Bouchard's campaign speech prior to the Quebec referendum in October 1995.

17 On the similarities between bantustans and reserves, see Bolaria and Li (1988), pages 70-71. In 1985 Glenn Babb, then South Africa's ambassador to Canada, himself made reference in a public speech to the apartheid regime's debt to Canada's reserves in formulating the bantustan policy.

18 On "white masculinity," see, among others, Sinha (1995) and Terkel (1992).

19 These places are contested spaces in Canada. They are sites of struggles over land claims, over treaty and non-treaty lands. Oka, where there was a police and military offensive against the indigenous peoples in 1990, is in Quebec. Gustafson Lake in British Columbia and Ipperwash in Ontario both saw struggles with the RCMP and provincial police in 1995, resulting in a death from police shooting in the latter.

20 Sophia Cook, a Jamaican-born 23-year-old single mother, was left with permanent injuries after being shot by Metro Toronto Police on October 27, 1989, when police stopped a car in which she was a passenger. The officer was charged with careless use of a firearm but was subsequently found not guilty.

21 Audrey Smith, a Jamaican woman visiting Toronto, was strip searched by Metro Toronto Police on a downtown street corner on August 10, 1993 on suspicion of having illegal drugs, although none were found in her possession.

22 On the history of multiculturalism, see Fleras and Elliot (1992).

23 For a discussion of this concept, see Habermas (1975).

24 For details of the French and English conquests of Canada and subsequent contestation between the two colonies, see Ryerson (1960) or Morton (1994). Quebec and English Canada have gone through a colonial relationship that, according to anglophone Canada or Ottawa, has been transformed into a liberal democratic incorporation. A vast portion of Quebec's population have, however, continued to perceive this as a modernized colonial relation.

25 The condition of crisis created by a state that is a white settler colony seeking to become a liberal democracy becomes clear when we look at Tester and Kulchyski (1994), who explore the genocidal consequences of Inuit relocation. There are numerous articles and books on the land claims issue. See, for example, Boldt and Long (1985).

26 On the transcendent nature of the state as an ideal democratic institution, see Miliband (1973).

27 On world system and dependency theories as readings of the First and Third Worlds in terms of capitalism, imperialism, and dependency, see Wallerstein (1979) and Gunder Frank (1978).

28 See Bolaria and Li (1988), chapters 2 and 3. This dynamic is explored in various ways by the Canadian Left nationalist political theorists, such as Teeple (1972). For a marxist critique of the Left nationalist position see Moore and Wells (1975).

29 This dependency is not simply a matter of adopting a British style of government (parliamentary democracy) or an American style of capitalism. Canada was a colony of Britain for a long time, and then, until recently, a dominion. Even now the Crown of England has a significant governmental relationship with the Canadian government. This is evident in the face of the Queen on Canadian currency or swearing allegiance to Her Majesty during citizenship ceremonies or in having to refer to the Crown and the House of Lords in matters of Native land claims. As for Canada's U.S. connection, political theorists of the Canadian Left such as Ian Lumsden, Mel Watkins, and others since the 1960s have drawn attention to a long-standing imperialist presence of U.S. capital in Canada. Canadian publishing, music, film, and cultural production and industry have been increasingly under attack from the U.S. culture industry and export market, and a steady dependency is being cultivated in the popular culture sector. This "Americanization" of Canadian culture has been both noticed and resented by writers such as Margaret Atwood or magazines such as *This Magazine* and *Canadian Dimension*.

30 See Law Union of Ontario (1981), as well as Canada (1974,1986).

31 See Bolaria and Li (1988), chapter 3.

32 For details on the Heritage Front and other neo-nazi/white supremacist groups, see *Hearts of Hate*, a video produced by the National Film Board and aired on the Canadian Broadcasting Corporation in 1995. An exposé carried in the *Toronto Star* in 1994 uncovered evidence that one of the founders of the Heritage Front, Grant Bristow, was a paid agent of the Canadian Security and Information Service (CSIS).

33 Regarding the concept of "survival," see Atwood (1972).

REFERENCES

Alexander, M. Jacqui, and Chandra Talpade Mohanty. "Introduction: Genealogies, Legacies, Movements," *in Feminist Genealogies, Colonial Legacies, Democratic Futures*, edited by M. Jacqui Alexander and Chandra Talpade Mohanty. New York/London: Routledge, 1997.

Allen, T. *The Invention of the White Race: Racial Oppression and Social Control.* London: Verso, 1994.

Althusser, L. *Lenin and Philosophy.* London: New Left Books, 1971.

Anderson, B. *Imagined Communities.* London: Verso, 1991.

Arnopoulos, S. *Problems of Immigrant Women in the Canadian Labour Force.* Ottawa: Canadian Advisory Council on the Status of Women, 1979.

Atwood, M. *Surfacing.* Toronto: McClelland & Stewart, 1972.

———. *Survival: A Thematic Guide to Canadian Literature.* Toronto: Anansi, 1972.

Avery, D. *Reluctant Host: Canada's Response to Immigrant Workers, 1896-1994.* Toronto: McClelland & Stewart, 1995.

Bolaria, B. S., and P. Li, eds. *Racial Oppression in Canada.* Toronto: Garamond, 1988.

Boldt, M., and J. A. Long, eds. *The Quest for Justice.* Toronto: University of Toronto Press, 1985.

Brand, D. *No Burden to Carry: Narratives of Black Working Women in Ontario, 1920s to 1950s.* Toronto: Women's Press, 1991.

Brand D., and K. S. Bhaggiyadatta, eds. *Rivers Have Sources, Trees Have Roots: Speaking of Racism.* Toronto: Cross Cultural Communications Centre, 1985.

Campbell, M. *Half Breed.* Toronto: Goodread Biographies, 1983.

Canada. *A Report of the Canadian Immigration and Population Study: Immigration Policy Perspective.* Ottawa: Manpower and Immigration, 1974.

———. *Equality Now: Report of the Special Committee on Visible Minorities.* Ottawa: House of Commons, 1986.

Carty, L., ed. *And Still We Rise.* Toronto: Women's Press, 1994.

Carty, L., and D. Brand. "Visible Minority Women: A Creation of the Colonial State," in *Returning the Gaze: Essays on Racism, Feminism and Politics,* edited by H. Bannerji. Toronto: Sister Vision Press, 1993.

Collins, P. H. *Black Feminist Thought: Knowledge, Consciousness and the Politics of Empowerment.* London: Harper Collins Academic, 1990.

Davis, A. *Women, Race and Class.* New York: Vintage, 1983.

Emberley, J. *Thresholds of Difference: Feminist Critique, Native Women's Writings, Postcolonial Theory.* Toronto: University of Toronto Press, 1993.

Fleras, A., and J. L. Elliot, eds. *Multiculturalism in Canada: The Challenge of Diversity.* Scarborough, Ont.: Nelson, 1992.

Francis, D. *The Imaginary Indian.* Vancouver: Arsenal Pulp Press, 1992.

Frankenberg, R. *White Women, Race Matters: The Social Construction of Whiteness.* Minneapolis: University of Minnesota Press, 1993.

Fraser, N., and L. Gordon. "A Genealogy of Dependency: A Keyword of the U.S. Welfare State." *Signs: A Journal of Women in Culture and Society* 19, no. 2 (1994): 309-36.

Goldberg, David T. *Racist Culture*. Oxford: Basil Blackwell, 1993.

Gunder Frank, Andre. *Dependent Accumulation and Underdevelopment*. London: Macmillan, 1978.

Habermas, J. *Legitimation Crisis*. Boston: Beacon, 1975.

hooks, b. *Ain't I a woman: black women and feminism*. Boston: South End Press, 1981.

Johnson, L., and R. Johnson. *Seam Allowance: Industrial Home Sewing in Canada*. Toronto: Women's Educational Press, 1982.

Kulchyski, P., ed. *Unjust Relations: Aboriginal Rights in Canadian Courts*. Toronto: Oxford University Press, 1994.

Law Union of Ontario. *The Immigrant's Handbook*. Montreal: Black Rose Books, 1981.

Macpherson, C.B. *Democratic Theory: Essays in Retrieval*. Oxford: Oxford University Press, 1973.

——. *The Life and Times of Liberal Democracy*. Toronto: Oxford University Press, 1977.

Miliband, Ralph. *The State in Capitalist Society: The Western System of Power*. London: Quartet Books, 1973.

Monture-Angus, P. *Thunder in My Soul: A Mohawk Woman Speaks*. Halifax: Fernwood, 1995.

Moore S., and D. Wells. *Imperialism and the National Question in Canada*. Toronto: Published by the authors, 1975.

Morton, Desmond. *A Short History of Canada*. Toronto: McClelland & Stewart, 1994.

Ng, R. "Sexism, Racism, Canadian Nationalism," in *Returning the Gaze: Essays on Racism, Feminism and Politics*, edited by H. Bannerji. Toronto: Sister Vision Press, 1993.

Roediger, D. *The Wages of Whiteness: Race and the Making of the American Working Class*. London: Verso, 1993.

Roman, Leslie G. "White is a Color: White Defensiveness, Postmodernism and Antiracist Pedagogy," in *Race, Identity and Representation in Education*, edited by C. McCarthy and W. Chrichlow. New York/London: Routledge, 1993.

Ryerson, Stanley. *The Foundation of Canada*. Toronto: Progress Books, 1960.

Sheehy, G. *The Silent Passage: Menopause*. New York: Pocket Books, 1991.

Silvera, M. *Silenced: Talks with Working Class Caribbean Women about Their Lives and Struggles as Domestic Workers in Canada* (2nd ed.). Toronto: Sister Vision Press, 1989.

Sinha, M. *Colonial Masculinity*. Manchester: Manchester University Press, 1995.

Smith, B. "Racism and Women's Studies," in *But Some of Us Are Brave*, edited by G. Hull, P. B. Scott, and B. Smith. New York: Feminist Press, 1982.

Smith, D. E. *The Everyday World as Problematic*. Toronto: University of Toronto Press, 1987.

———. *The Conceptual Practices of Power: A Feminist Sociology of Knowledge*. Toronto: University of Toronto Press, 1990.

Stoller, A. L. *Race and the Education of Desire: Foucault's History of Sexuality and the Colonial Order of Things*. Durham: Duke University Press, 1995.

Teeple, G., ed. *Capitalism and the National Question*. Toronto: University of Toronto Press, 1972.

Terkel, S. *Race: How Blacks and Whites Think and Feel about the American Obsession*. New York: The New Press, 1992.

Tester, F. J., and P. Kulchyski. *Tammarniit (Mistakes): Innuit Relocation in the Eastern Arctic*. Vancouver: University of British Columbia Press, 1994.

Wallerstein, Immanuel. *Capitalist World Economy*. London: Cambridge University Press, 1979.

Ware, V. *Beyond the Pale: White Women, Racism, and History*. London: Verso, 1991.

Watkins, M., ed. *Dene Nation: The Colony Within*. Toronto: University of Toronto Press, 1977.

Watson, S. "Race, Wilderness, Territory and the Origins of Modern Canadian Landscape Painting," *Semiotext[e]* 6, no. 17 (1994): 93-104.

CHAPTER 3

On the Dark Side of the Nation:
Politics of Multiculturalism
and the State of "Canada"

*T*his paper is primarily concerned with the construction of "Canada" as a social and cultural form of national identity, and various challenges and interruptions offered to this identity by literature produced by writers from non-white communities. The first part of the paper examines both literary and political-theoretical formulations of a "two-nation," "two solitudes" thesis and their implications for various cultural accommodations offered to "others," especially through the mechanism of "multiculturalism." The second part concentrates on the experiences and standpoint of people of colour, or non-white people, especially since the 1960s, and the cultural and political formulating derivable from them.

> I am from the country
> Columbus dreamt of.
> You, the country
> Columbus conquered.
> Now in your land
> My words are circling
> blue Oka sky
> they come back to us
> alight on tongue.

Protect me with your brazen passion
for history is my truth,
Earth, my witness
my home,
this native land.

"OKA NADA": *A New Remembrance*
Kaushalya Bannerji (1993, p. 20)

THE PERSONAL AND THE POLITICAL:
A CHORUS AND A PROBLEMATIC

When the women's movement came along and we were coming to
our political consciousness, one of its slogans took us by surprise
and thrilled and activated us: "the personal is political!" Since then
years have gone by, and in the meanwhile I have found myself in
Canada, swearing an oath of allegiance to the Queen of England,
giving up the passport of a long-fought-for independence, and being
assigned into the category of "visible minority." These years have
produced their own consciousness in me, and I have learnt that
also the reverse is true: the political is personal.

The way this consciousness was engendered was not
ideological, but daily, practical and personal. It came from having
to live within an all-pervasive presence of the state in our everyday
life. It began with the Canadian High Commission's rejection of
my two-year-old daughter's visa and continued with my airport
appearance in Montreal, where I was interrogated at length. What
shook me was not the fact that they interviewed me, but rather
their tone of suspicion about my somehow having stolen my way
"in."

As the years progressed, I realized that in my life, and in the
lives of other non-white people around me, this pervasive presence
of the state meant everything — allowing my daughter and husband
to come into the country; permitting me to continue my studies or
to work, to cross the border into the U.S.A. and back; allowing me
the custody of my daughter, although I had a low income; "landing"

me so I could put some sort of life together with some predictability. Fear, anxiety, humiliation, anger and frustration became the wire-mesh that knit bits of my life into a pattern. The quality of this life may be symbolized by an incident with which my final immigration interview culminated after many queries about a missing "wife" and the "head of the family." I was facing an elderly, bald, white man, moustached and blue-eyed — who said he had been to India. I made some polite rejoinder and he asked me — "Do you speak Hindi?" I replied that I understood it very well and spoke it with mistakes. "Can you translate this sentence for me?" he asked, and proceeded to say in Hindi what in English amounts to "Do you want to fuck with me?" A wave of heat rose from my toes to my hair roots. I gripped the edge of my chair and stared at him — silently. His hand was on my passport, the pink slip of my "landing" document lay next to it. Steadying my voice I said "I don't know Hindi that well." "So you're a PhD student?" My interview continued. I sat rigid and concluded it with a schizophrenic intensity. On Bloor Street in Toronto, sitting on the steps of a church — I vomited. I was a landed immigrant.

Throughout these twenty-five years I have met many non-white and Third World legal and illegal "immigrants" and "new Canadians" who feel that the machinery of the state has us impaled against its spikes. In beds, in workplaces, in suicides committed over deportations, the state silently, steadily rules our lives with "regulations." How much more intimate could we be — this state and we? It has almost become a person — this machinery — growing with and into our lives, fattened with our miseries and needs, and the curbing of our resistance and anger.

But simultaneously with the growth of the state we grew too, both in numbers and protest, and became a substantial voting population in Canada. We demanded some genuine reforms, some changes — some among us even demanded the end of racist capitalism — and instead we got "multiculturalism." "Communities" and their leaders or representatives were created by and through the state, and they called for funding and promised "essential services" for their "communities," such as the preservation of their identities. There were advisory bodies, positions, and even arts

funding created on the basis of ethnicity and community. A problem
of naming arose, and hyphenated cultural and political identities
proliferated. Officially constructed identities came into being and
we had new names — immigrant, visible minority, new Canadian
and ethnic. In the mansion of the state small back rooms were
accorded to these new political players on the scene. Manoeuvring
for more began. As the state came deeper into our lives — extending
its political, economic and moral regulation, its police violence and
surveillance — we simultaneously officialized ourselves. It is as
though we asked for bread and were given stones, and could not
tell the difference between the two.

IN OR OF THE NATION?
THE PROBLEM OF BELONGING

Face it there's an illegal
Immigrant
Hiding in your house
Hiding in you
Trying to get out!
* * * *

Businessmen Custom's officials
Dark Glasses Industrial Aviation
Policemen Illegal Bachelorettes
Sweatshop-Keepers Information Canada
Says
"You can't get their smell off
the walls."

Domestic Bliss
Krisantha Sri Bhaggiyadatta (1981, p. 23)

The state and the "visible minorities," (the non-white people living
in Canada) have a complex relationship with each other. There is a
fundamental unease with how our difference is construed and
constructed by the state, how our otherness in relation to Canada
is projected and objectified. We cannot be successfully ingested, or

assimilated, or made to vanish from where we are not wanted. We remain an ambiguous presence, our existence a question mark in the side of the nation, with the potential to disclose much about the political unconscious and consciousness of Canada as an "imagined community" (Anderson, 1991). Disclosures accumulate slowly, while we continue to live here as outsider-insiders of the nation which offers a proudly multicultural profile to the international community. We have the awareness that we have arrived into somebody's state, but what kind of state; whose imagined community or community of imagination does it embody? And what are the terms and conditions of our "belonging" to this state of a nation? Answers to these questions are often indirect and not found in the news highway of Canadian media. But travelling through the side-roads of political discursivities and practices we come across markers for social terrains and political establishments that allow us to map the political geography of this nation-land where we have "landed."

We locate our explorations of Canada mainly in that part where compulsorily English-speaking visible minorities reside, a part renamed by Charles Taylor and others as "Canada outside of Quebec" (COQ).[1] But we will call it "English Canada" as in common parlance. This reflects the binary cultural identity of the country to whose discourse, through the notions of the two solitudes, survival and bilingualism, "new comers" are subjected.[2] Conceptualizing Canada within this discourse is a bleak and grim task: since "solitude" and "survival" (with their Hobbesian and Darwinist aura) are hardly the language of communitarian joy in nation making.

What, I asked when I first heard of these solitudes, are they? And why survival, when Canada's self-advertisement is one of a wealthy industrial nation? Upon my immigrant inquiries these two solitudes turned out to be two invading European nations — the French and the English — which might have produced two colonial-nation states in this part of North America. But history did not quite work out that way. Instead of producing two settler colonial countries like Zimbabwe (Rhodesia) and South Africa, they held a relationship of conquest and domination with each other. After the battle at the Plains of Abraham one conquered nation/nationality, the French, continued in an uneasy and subjected relation to a state of "Canada," which they saw as "English," a perception ratified by this state's rootedness in the English Crown. The colonial French then came to a hyphenated identity of "franco-something," or declared themselves (at least within one province) as plain "Québécois." They have been existing ever since in an unhappy state, their promised status as a "distinct society" notwithstanding. Periodically, and at times critically, Quebec challenges "Canadian" politics of "unity" and gives this politics its own "distinct" character. These then are the two solitudes, the protagonists who, to a great extent, shape the ideological parameters of Canadian constitutional debates, and whose "survival" and relations are continually deliberated. And this preoccupation is such a "natural" of Canadian politics that all other inhabitants are only a minor part of the problematic of "national" identity. This is particularly evident in the role, or lack thereof, accorded to the First Nations of Canada in the nation-forming project. Even after Elijah Harper's intervention in the Meech Lake Accord, the deployment of the Canadian Army against the Mohawk peoples and the long stand-off that followed, constant land claims and demands for self government/self-determination, there is a remarkable and a determined political marginalization of the First Nations. And yet their presence as the absent signifiers within Canadian national politics works at all times as a bedrock of its national definitional project, giving it a very particular contour through the same absences, silences, exclusions and marginalizations. In this there is no distinction between "COQ" or English Canada and Quebec. One needs only to look at the siege at Oka to realize that as far as these "others" are concerned, Europeans continue the same solidarity of ruling and repression, blended with competitive manipulations, that they practiced from the dawn of their conquests and state formations.

The Anglo-French rivalry therefore needs to be read through the lens of colonialism. If we want to understand the relationship between visible minorities and the state of Canada/English Canada/COQ, colonialism is the context or entry point that allows us to begin exploring the social relations and cultural forms which characterize these relations. The construction of visible minorities as a social imaginary and the architecture of the "nation" built with a "multicultural mosaic" can only be read together with the engravings of conquests, wars and exclusions. It is the nationhood of this Canada, with its two solitudes and their survival anxieties and aggressions against "native others," that provides the epic painting in whose dark corners we must look for the later "others." We have to get past and through these dual monoculturalist assumptions or paradigms in order to speak about "visible minorities," a category produced by the multiculturalist policy of the state. This paper repeats, in its conceptual and deconstructive movements, the motions of the people themselves who, "appellated" as refugees, immigrants or visible minorities, have to file past immigration officers, refugee boards, sundry ministries and posters of multi-featured/coloured faces that blandly proclaim "Together we are Ontario" — lest we or they forget!

We will examine the assumptions of "Canada" from the conventional problematic and thematic of Canadian nationhood, that of '"Fragmentation or Integration?" currently resounding in post-referendum times. I look for my place within this conceptual topography and find myself in a designated space for "visible minorities in the multicultural society and state of Canada." This is existence in a zone somewhere between economy and culture. It strikes me then that this discursive mode in which Canada is topicalized does not anywhere feature the concept of class. Class does not function as a potential source for the theorization of Canada, any more than does race as an expression for basic social relations of contradiction. Instead the discursivities rely on hegemonic cultural categories such as English or French Canada, or on notions such as national institutions, and conceive of differences and transcendences, fragmentation and integration, with regard to an ideological notion of unity that is perpetually in crisis. This influential problematic is displayed in a *Globe and Mail* editorial of 29 March 1994. It is typically pre-occupied with themes of unity and integration or fragmentation, and delivers a lecture on these to Lucien Bouchard of the Bloc Québécois.

> It has been an educational field trip for Lucien Bouchard. On his
> first venture into "English Canada" (as he insists on calling it)

since becoming leader of Her Majesty's Loyal Opposition, Mr.
Bouchard learned, among other things, there is such a thing as
Canadian Nationalism: not just patriotism, nor yet that self-serving
little prejudice that parades around as Canadian Nationalism —
mix equal parts elitism, statism and Anti-Americanism — but a
genuine fellow-feeling that binds Canadians to one another across
this country — and includes Quebec.

Lest this statement appear to the people of Quebec as passing off
"English Canada" disguised as "the nation" and locking Quebec in
a vice grip of "unity" without consent or consultation, the editor
repeats multiculturalist platitudes meant to mitigate the old
antagonisms leading to "separatism." The demand for a French
Canada is equated with, "self-serving little prejudice" and
"patriotism," and promptly absorbed into the notion of a culturally
and socially transcendent Canada, which is supposedly not only
non-French, but non-English as well. How can this non-partisan,
transcendent Canada be articulated except in the discourse of
multiculturalism? Multiculturalism, then, can save the day for
English Canada, conferring upon it a transcendence, even though
the same transcendent state is signalled through the figure of Her
Majesty the Queen of England and the English language. The
unassimilable "others" who, in their distance from English Canada,
need to be boxed into this catch-all phrase now become the moral
cudgel with which to beat Quebec's separatist aspirations. The same
editorial continues:

> Canada is dedicated to the ideal that people of different languages
> and cultures may, without surrendering their identity, yet embrace
> the human values they have in common: the "two solitudes" of
> which the poet wrote, "that protect and touch and greet each
> other," were a definition of love, not division.

But this poetic interpretation of solitudes, like the moral carrot of
multicultural love is quickly followed by a stick. Should Quebec
not recognize this obligation to love, but rather see it as a barrier
to self-determination, Canada will not tolerate this. We are then

confronted with other competing self-determinations in one breath, some of which ordinarily would not find their advocate in *Globe and Mail* editorials. What of the self-determination of the Cree, of the anglophones, of federalists of every stripe? What of the self-determination of the Canadian nation? Should Mr. Bouchard and his kind not recognize this national interest, it is argued, then the province's uncertainties are only beginning. In the context of the editorial's discourse, these uncertainties amount to the threat of a federalist anglophone war. The "self-determination of the Cree" is no more than an opportunistic legitimation of Canada in the name of all others who are routinely left out of its construction and governance. These "different (from the French) others," through the device of a state-sponsored multiculturalism, create the basis for transcendence necessary for the creation of a universalist liberal democratic statehood. They are interpellated or bound into the ideological state apparatus through their employment of tongues which must be compulsorily, officially unilingual — namely, under the sign of English.[3]

"Canada," with its primary inscriptions of "French" or "English," its colonialist and essentialist identity markers, cannot escape a fragmentary framework. Its imagined political geography simplifies into two primary and confrontational possessions, cultural typologies and dominant ideologies. Under the circumstances, all appeal to multiculturalism on the part of "Canada Outside Quebec" becomes no more than an extra weight on the "English" side. Its "difference-studded unity," its "multicultural mosaic," becomes an ideological sleight of hand pitted against Quebec's presumably greater cultural homogeneity. The two solitudes glare at each other from the barricades in an ongoing colonial war. But what do either of these solitudes and their reigning essences have to do with those whom the state has named "visible minorities" and who are meant to provide the ideological basis for the Canadian state's liberal/ universal status? How does their very "difference," inscribed with inferiority and negativity — their otherwise troublesome particularity — offer the very particularist state of "English Canada" the legitimating device of transcendence through multiculturalism? Are we not still being used in the war between the English and the French?

It may seem strange to "Canadians" that the presence of the First Nations, the "visible minorities" and the ideology of multiculturalism are being suggested as the core of the state's claim to universality or transcendence. Not only in multiplying pawns in the old Anglo-French rivalry but in other ways as well, multiculturalism may be seen less as a gift of the state of "Canada" to the "others" of this society, than as a central pillar in its own ideological state apparatus.[4] This is because the very discourse of nationhood in the context of "Canada," given its evolution as a capitalist state derived from a white settler colony with aspirations to liberal democracy,[5] needs an ideology that can mediate fissures and ruptures more deep and profound than those of the usual capitalist nation state.[6] That is why usually undesirable others, consisting of non-white peoples with their ethnic or traditional or underdeveloped cultures, are discursively inserted in the middle of a dialogue on hegemonic rivalry. The discourse of multiculturalism, as distinct from its administrative, practical relations and forms of ruling, serves as a culmination for the ideological construction of "Canada." This places us, on whose actual lives the ideology is evoked, in a peculiar situation. On the one hand, by our sheer presence we provide a central part of the distinct pluralist unity of Canadian nationhood; on the other hand, this centrality is dependent on our "difference," which denotes the power of definition that "Canadians" have over "others." In the ideology of multicultural nationhood, however, this difference is read in a power-neutral manner rather than as organized through class, gender and race. Thus at the same moment that difference is ideologically evoked it is also neutralized, as though the issue of difference were the same as that of diversity of cultures and identities, rather than that of racism and colonial ethnocentrism — as though our different cultures were on a par or could negotiate with the two dominant ones! The hollowness of such a pluralist stance is exposed in the shrill indignation of anglophones when rendered a "minority" in Quebec, or the angry desperation of francophones in Ontario. The issue of the First Nations — their land claims, languages and cultures — provides another dimension entirely, so violent and deep that the state of Canada dare not even name it in the placid language of multiculturalism.

The importance of the discourse of multiculturalism to that of nation-making becomes clearer if we remember that "nation" needs an ideology of unification and legitimation.[7] As Benedict Anderson points out, nations need to imagine a principle of "com-unity," or community even where there is little there to postulate any.[8] A nation, ideologically, can not posit itself on the principle of hate, according to Anderson, and must therefore speak to the sacrificing of individual, particularist interests for the sake of "the common good" (1991, ch. 2). This task of "imagining community" becomes especially difficult in Canada — not only because of class, gender and capital, which ubiquitously provide contentious grounds in the most culturally homogeneous of societies — but because its socio-political space is saturated by elements of surplus domination due to its Eurocentric/racist/colonial context. Ours is not a situation of co-existence of cultural nationalities or tribes within a given geographical space. Speaking here of culture without addressing power relations displaces and trivializes deep contradictions. It is a reductionism that hides the social relations of domination that continually create "difference" as inferior and thus signifies continuing relations of antagonism. The legacy of a white settler colonial economy and state and the current aspirations to imperialist capitalism mark Canada's struggle to become a liberal democratic state. Here a cultural pluralist interpretive discourse hides more than it reveals. It serves as a fantastic evocation of "unity," which in any case becomes a reminder of the divisions. Thus to imagine "com-unity" means to imagine a common-project of valuing difference that would hold good for both Canadians and others, while also claiming that the sources of these otherizing differences are merely cultural. As that is impossible, we consequently have a situation where no escape is possible from divisive social relations. The nation state's need for an ideology that can avert a complete rupture becomes desperate, and gives rise to a multicultural ideology which both needs and creates "others" while subverting demands for anti-racism and political equality.

Let me illustrate my argument by means of Charles Taylor's thoughts on the Canadian project of nation making. Taylor is comparable to Benedict Anderson insofar as he sees "nation" primarily as an expression of civil society, as a collective form of self-determination and definition. He therefore sees that culture, community, tradition and imagination are crucial for this process. His somewhat romantic organicist approach is pitted against neo-liberal projects of market ideologies misnamed as "reform."[9] Taylor draws his inspiration, among many sources, from an earlier European romantic tradition that cherishes cultural specificities, local traditions and imaginations.[10] This presents Taylor with the difficult task of "reconciling solitudes" with some form of a state while retaining traditional cultural identities in an overall ideological circle of "Canadian" nationhood. This is a difficult task at all times, but especially in the Canadian context of Anglo-French rivalry and the threat of separatism. Thus Taylor, in spite of his philosophical refinement, is like others also forced into the recourse of "multiculturalism as a discourse," characterized by its reliance on diversity. The constitution then becomes a federal Mosaic tablet for encoding and enshrining this very moral/political mandate. But Taylor is caught in a further bind, because Canada is more than a dual monocultural entity. Underneath the "two solitudes," as he knows well, Canada has "different differences," a whole range of cultural identities which cannot (and he feels should not) be given equal status with the "constituent elements" of "the nation," namely, the English and the French. At this point Taylor has to juggle with the contending claims of these dominant or "constituent" communities and their traditions, with the formal equality of citizenship in liberal democracy, and with other "others" with their contentious political claims and "different cultures." This juggling, of course, happens best in a multicultural language, qualifying the claim of the socio-economic equality of "others" with the language of culture and tolerance, converting difference into diversity in order to mitigate the power relations underlying it. Thus Taylor, in spite of his organicist, communitarian-moral view of the nation and the state, depends on a modified liberal pluralist discourse which he otherwise finds "American," abstract, empty and unpalatable.[11]

Reconciling the Solitudes and Multiculturalism and the Politics of Recognition are important texts for understanding the need for the construction of the category of visible minorities to manage contentions in the nationhood of Canada. Even though Taylor spends little time actually discussing either the visible minorities or the First Nations, their importance for the creation of a national ideology is brought out by his discussion of Anglo-French contestation. Their visceral anxieties about loss of culture are offset by "other" cultural presences that are minoritized with respect to both, while the commonality of Anglo-French culture emerges in contrast. Taylor discovers that the cultural essences of COQ have something in common with Quebec — their Europeanness — in spite of the surface of diversity. This surface diversity, he feels, is not insurmountable within the European-Anglo framework, whose members' political imagination holds enough ground for some sort of commonality.

> What is enshrined here is what one might call *first level diversity*. There are great differences in culture and outlook and background in a population that nevertheless shares the same idea of what it is to belong to Canada. Their patriotism and manner of belonging is uniform, whatever their differences, and this is felt to be necessary if the country is to hold together. (1993, p. 182)

Taylor must be speaking of those who are "Canadians" and not "others": the difference of visible minorities and First Nations peoples is obviously not containable in this "first level diversity" category. As far as these "others" are concerned the Anglo-European (COQ) and French elements have much in common in both "othering" and partially "tolerating" them. Time and time again, especially around the so-called Oka crisis, it became clear that liberal pluralism rapidly yields to a fascist "sons of the soil" approach as expressed by both the Quebec state and its populace, oblivious to the irony of such a claim. It is inconsistent of Taylor to use this notion of "first level diversity" while also emphasizing the irreducible cultural ontology of Quebec as signaled by the concept of a "deep diversity" (p. 183). But more importantly, this inconsistency accords an ownership of nationhood to the Anglo-French elements. He wrestles, therefore, to accommodate an Anglo-French nationality, while the "deep diversities" of "others," though nominally cited, are erased from the political map just as easily as the similarity of the "two nations" *vis-à-vis* those "others." Of course, these manipulations are essential for Taylor and others if the European (colonial) character of "Canada" is to be held *status quo*. This is a Trudeau-like stance of dual unification in which non-European "others" are made to lend support to the enterprise by their existence as a tolerated managed difference.

This multicultural take on liberal democracy, called the "politics of recognition" by Taylor, is informed by his awareness that an across-the-board use of the notion of equality would reduce the French element from the status of "nation" to that of just another minority. This of course must not be allowed to happen, since the French are, by virtue of being European co-conquerors, one of the "founding nations." At this point Taylor adopts the further qualified notion of visible minorities as integral to his two-in-one nation-state schema. For him as for other majority ideologues they constitute a minority of minorities. They are, in the scheme of things, peripheral to the essence of Canada, which is captured by "Trudeau's remarkable achievement in extending bilingualism" to reflect the "Canadian" character of "duality" (p. 164). This duality Taylor considers as currently under a threat of irrelevancy, not from anglo monoculturism, but from the ever-growing presence of "other" cultures. "Already one hears Westerners saying…that their experience of Canada is of a multicultural mosaic" (p. 182). This challenge of the presence of "others" is, for Taylor, the main problem for French Canadians in retaining their equality with English Canadians. But it is also a problem for Taylor himself, who sees in this an unsettling possibility for the paradigm of "two solitudes" or "two nations" to which he ultimately concedes. In order to project and protect the irreducible claims of the two dominant and similar cultures, he refers fleetingly and analogically, though frequently, to aboriginal communities: "visible minorities" also enter his discourse, but both are terms serving to install a "national" conversation between French and English, embroidering the dialogue of the main speakers. His placement of these "other" social groups is evident when he says: "Something analogous [to the French situation] holds for aboriginal communities in this country; their way of being Canadian is not accommodated by first level diversity" (p. 182). Anyone outside of the national framework adopted by Taylor would feel puzzled by the analogical status of the First Nations brought in to negotiate power sharing between the two European nations. Taylor's approach is in keeping with texts on nationalism, culture and identity that relegate the issues of colonialism, racism and continued oppression of the Aboriginal peoples and the oppression visited upon "visible minorities" to the status of footnotes in Canadian politics.

Yet multiculturalism as an ideological device both enhances and erodes Taylor's project. Multiculturalism, he recognizes at one level, is plain realism — an effect of the realization that many (perhaps too many) "others" have been allowed in, stretching the skin of tolerance and "first level diversity" tightly across the body of the nation. Their "deep diversity" cannot be accommodated simply within the Anglo-French duality. The situation is so murky that, "more fundamentally" we face a challenge to our very conception of diversity" (p. 182). "Difference," he feels, has to be more "fundamentally" read into the "nation":

> In a way, accommodating difference is what Canada is all about. Many Canadians would concur in this. (p. 181)
>
> Many of the people who rallied around the Charter and multiculturalism to reject the distinct society are proud of their acceptance of diversity — and in some respects rightly so. (p. 182)

But this necessary situational multiculturalism acknowledged by Taylor not only creates the transcendence of a nation built on difference, it also introduces the claims of "deep diversities" on all sides. Unable to formulate a way out of this impasse Taylor proposes an ideological utopia of "difference" (devoid of the issue of power) embodied in a constitutional state, a kind of cultural federalism:

> To build a country for everyone, Canada would have to allow for second-level or "deep" diversity in which a plurality of ways of belonging would also be acknowledged and accepted. Someone of, say, Italian extraction in Toronto or Ukrainian extraction in

Edmonton might indeed feel Canadian as a bearer of individual rights in a multicultural mosaic. His or her belonging would not "pass through" some other community, although the ethnic identity might be important to him or her in various ways. But this person might nevertheless accept that a Québécois or a Cree or a Dene might belong in a very different way, that these persons were Canadian through being members of their national communities. Reciprocally, the Québécois, Cree, or Dene would accept the perfect legitimacy of the "mosaic" identity. (p. 183)

This utopian state formation of Taylor founders, as do those of others, on the rocky shores of the reality of how different "differences" are produced, or are not just forms of diversity. For all of Taylor's pleas for recognizing two kinds of diversity, he does not ever probe into the social relations of power that create the different differences. It is perhaps significant from this point of view that he speaks of the "deep diversities" of Italians or Ukrainians but does not mention those of the blacks, South Asians or the Chinese. In other words, he cannot raise the spectre of real politics, of real social, cultural and economic relations of white supremacy and racism. Thus he leaves out of sight the relations and ideologies of ruling that are intrinsic to the creation of a racist civil society and a racializing colonial-liberal state. It is this foundational evasion that makes Taylor's proposal so problematic for those whose "differences" in the Canadian context are not culturally intrinsic but constructed through "race," class, gender and other relations of power. This is what makes us sceptical about Taylor's retooling of multicultural liberal democracy by introducing the concept of "deep diversity" as a differentiated citizenship into the bone marrow of the polity, while leaving the Anglo-French European "national" (colonial and racist) core intact. He disagrees with those for whom

...[the] model of citizenship has to be uniform, or [they think] people would have no sense of belonging to the same polity. Those who say so tend to take the United States as their paradigm, which has indeed been hostile to deep diversity and has sometimes tried to stamp it out as "un-American." (p. 183)

This, for Taylor, amounts to the creation of a truly Canadian polity that needs a "united federal Canada" and is able to deliver "law and order, collective provision, regional equality and mutual self help..." (p. 183). None of these categories — for example, that of "law and order" — is characteristically problematized by Taylor. His model "Canada" is not to be built on the idea of a melting pot or of a uniform citizenship based on a rationalist and functional view of polity. That would, according to him, "straight-jacket" deep diversity. Instead,

> The world needs other models to be legitimated in order to allow for more humane and less constraining modes of political cohabitation. Instead of pushing ourselves to the point of break up in the name of a uniform model, we would do our own and some other peoples a favour by exploring the space of deep diversity. (p. 184)

What would this differentiated citizenship look like in concrete example, we ask? Taylor throws in a few lines about Basques, Catalans and Bretons. But those few lines are not answer enough for us. Though this seems to be an open invitation to join the project of state and nation making, the realities of a colonial capitalist history — indentures, reserves, First Nations without a state, immigrants and citizens, illegals, refugees and "Canadians" — make it impossible. They throw us against the inscription of power-based "differences" that construct the self-definition of the Canadian state and its citizenship. We realize that class, "race," gender, sexual orientation, colonialism and capital can not be made to vanish by the magic of Taylor's multiculturalism, managed and graduated around a core of dualism. His inability to address current and historical organizations of power, his inability to see that this sort of abstract and empty invitation to "difference" has always enhanced the existing "difference" unless real social equality and historical redress can be possible — these erasures make his proposal a touch frightening for us. This is why I shudder to "take the deep road of diversity together" with Charles Taylor (p. 184). Concentration and labour camps, Japanese internment, the Indian

Act and reserves, apartheid and ethnic "homelands" extend their
long shadows over the project of my triumphal march into the
federal utopia of a multiculturally differentiated citizenship. But
what becomes clear from Taylor's writings is the importance of a
discourse of difference and multiculturalism for the creation of a
legitimate nation space for Canada. Multiculturalism becomes a
mandate of moral regulation as an antidote to any, and especially
Quebec's, separatism.

ON THE DARK SIDE OF THE NATION:
CONSIDERING "ENGLISH CANADA"

If one stands on the dark side of the nation in Canada everything
looks different. The transcendent, universal and unifying claims of
its multiculturally legitimated ideological state apparatus become
susceptible to questions. The particularized and partisan nature of
this nation-state becomes visible through the same ideological and
working apparatus that simultaneously produces its national
"Canadian" essence and the "other" — its non-white population
(minus the First Nations) as "visible minorities." It is obvious that
both Canada and its adjectivized correlates English or French
Canada are themselves certain forms of constructions. What do
these constructions represent or encode? With regard to whom or
what are we otherized and categorized as visible minorities? What
lies on the dark side of this state project, its national ethos?

Official multiculturalism, mainstream political thought and the
news media in Canada all rely comfortably on the notion of a nation
and its state both called Canada, with legitimate subjects called
Canadians, in order to construct us as categorical forms of
difference. There is an assumption that this Canada is a singular
entity, a moral, cultural and political essence, neutral of power,
both in terms of antecedents and consequences. The assumption is
that we can recognize this beast, if and when we see it. So we can
then speak of a "Pan-Canadian nationalism," of a Canada which
will not tolerate more Third World immigrants or separatism, or
of what Canada needs or allows us to do. And yet, when we
scrutinize this Canada, what is it that we see? The answer to this

question depends on which side of the nation we inhabit. For those who see it as a homogeneous cultural/political entity, resting on a legitimately possessed territory, with an exclusive right to legislation over diverse groups of peoples, Canada is unproblematic. For others, who are on the receiving end of the power of Canada and its multiculturalism, who have been dispossessed in one sense or another, the answer is quite different. For them the issues of legitimacy of territorial possession, or the right to create regulations and the very axis of domination on which its status as a nation-state rests, are all too central to be pushed aside. To them the same Canada appears as a post-conquest capitalist state, economically dependent on an imperialist United States and politically implicated in English and U.S. imperialist enterprises, with some designs of its own. From this perspective "Pan-Canadianism" loses its transcendent inclusivity and emerges instead as a device and a legitimation for a highly particularized ideological form of domination. Canada then becomes mainly an English Canada, historicized into particularities of its actual conquerors and their social and state formations. Colonialism remains as a vital formational and definitional issue. Canada, after all, could not be English or French in the same sense in which England and France are English and French.

Seen thus, the essence of Canada is destabilized. It becomes a politico-military ideological construction and constitution, elevating aggressive acts of acquisition and instituting them into a formal stabilization. But this stability is tenuous, always threatening to fall apart. The adjective "English" stamped into "Canada" bares this reality, both past and present. It shows us who stands on the other side of the "Pan-Canadian" project. Quebeckers know it well, and so their colonial rivalry continues. And we, the "visible minorities" — multiculturalism notwithstanding — know our equidistance from both of these conquering essences. The issue at stake, in the end, is felt by all sides to be much more than cultural. It is felt to be about the power to define what is Canada or Canadian culture. This power can only come through the actual possession of a geographical territory and the economy of a nation-state. It is this which confers the legal imprimatur to define what is Canadian or French Canadian, or what are "sub"- or "multi"-cultures. Bilingualism, multiculturalism, tolerance of diversity and difference and slogans of unity cannot solve this problem of unequal power and exchange — except to entrench even further the social relations of power and their ideological and legal forms, which emanate from an unproblematized Canadian state and essence. What discursive magic can vanish a continuously proliferating process of domination and thus of marginalization and oppression? What can make it a truly multicultural state when all the power relations and the signifiers of Anglo-French white supremacy are barely concealed behind a straining liberal democratic façade?

The expression "white supremacist,"[12] harsh and shocking as it may sound to many, encodes the painful underpinnings of the category visible minorities. The ideological imperatives of other categories — such as immigrants, aliens, foreigners, ethnic communities or New Canadians — constellate around the same binary code. There is a direct connection between this and the ideological spin-off of Englishness or Frenchness. After all, if nations are "imagined communities," can the content of this national imagination called Canada be free of its history and current social relations of power? Does not the context inflect the content here and now?

At this point we need to remind ourselves that there are different kinds of nationalisms — some aggressive and others assertive. Benedict Anderson makes a useful distinction between an "official nationalism" of imperialism, and the "popular nationalism" of lived relations of a settled society and its shared historical/cultural relations (1991, p. 86).[13] The former, Anderson claims, is about hate and aggression; the latter, about love and sacrifice of a people for a shared culture, ancestral history and a shared physical space. This "popular nationalism" in my view is clearly not possible for Canada, whose context is the colonization and continued marginalization of the First Nations while seeking to build a liberal democratic state. In Canada, such "popular nationalism" contains legal/coercive strategies and the means of containment and suppression of all "others." The kinship or blood-ties of which Anderson speaks as elements of a nation are ranged along two contending sides (p. 19). On the side of Canada there is a history and kinship of European/English colonial and subsequently

American complicity in domination, of bad faith and broken promises and at best, of guilt. On the other side is the labour-migration kinship of all who stand in the underside of this Canada, roped in by relations of colonialism and imperialism with their race-gender and cultural discrimination. This European domination is coded as "civilized" and "modernizing" and signified through "white,"[14] while global resistance or acquiescence to them are carried on by "others" who are colour coded as "visible," meaning non-white, black or dark.

The case of Canada and its nationalism, when considered in this light, is not very different from the "official nationalism" of South Africa, erstwhile Rhodesia, or of Australia. These are cases of colonial "community" in which nation and state formations were created through the conquering imagination of white supremacy.[15] An anxiety about "them" — the aboriginals, pre-existing people — provides the core of a fantasy which inverts the colonized into aggressors, resolving the problem through extermination, suppression and containment.[16] Dominant cultural language in every one of these countries resounds with an "us" and "them" as expressed through discursivities of "minority/sub/multi-culture." A thinly veiled, older colonial discourse of civilization and savagery peeps out from the modern versions. Here difference is not a simple marker of cultural diversity, but rather, measured or constructed in terms of distance from civilizing European cultures. Difference here is branded always with inferiority or negativity. This is displayed most interestingly in the reading of the non-white or dark body which is labelled as a visible and minority body.[17] The colour of the skin, facial and bodily features — all become signifiers of inferiority, composed of an inversion and a projection of what is considered evil by the colonizing society. Implied in these cultural constructions is a literal denigration, extending into a valorized expression of European racist-patriarchy coded as white.

This inscription of whiteness underwrites whatever may be called Englishness, Frenchness, and finally Europeanness. These national characteristics become moral ones and they spin off or spill over into each other. Thus whiteness extends into moral qualities of masculinity, possessive individualism and an ideology of capital and market.[18] They are treated as indicators of civilization,

freedom and modernity. The inherent aggressiveness and asociality
of this moral category "whiteness" derives its main communitarian
aspect from an animosity towards "others," signaling the
militaristic, elite and otherizing bond shared by conquerors. The
notion of Englishness serves as a metaphor for whiteness, as do all
other European national essences. Whiteness, as many have noted,
thus works as an ideology of a nation-state. It can work most
efficiently with an other/enemy in its midst, constantly inventing
new signifiers of "us" and "them." In the case of Canada the others,
the First Nations, have been there from the very inception,
modulating the very formation of its state and official culture,
constantly presenting them with doubts about their legitimacy.
Subsequently, indentured workers, immigrants, refugees and other
"others" have only deepened this legitimation crisis, though they
also helped to forge the course of the state and the "nation."[19]
"English," as an official language, has served to create a hegemonic
front, but it is not a powerful enough antidote as an ideological
device to undermine antagonisms that are continually created
through processes of ruling; it is the ideology of "whiteness/
Europeanness" that serves as the key bonding element. Even though
the shame of being an Italian, that is, non-English, in Canada
outweighs the glory of the Italian renaissance, "Italian" can still
form a part of the community of "whiteness" as distinct from non-
white "others." It is not surprising, therefore, to see that one key
element of white supremacy in Canada was an "Orange" mentality
connecting Englishness with whiteness and both with racial purity.
Books such as Shades of Right, for example, speak precisely to this,
as does the present day right-wing nationalism of "English"-based
groups. Quebec's "French" nationalism has precisely the same
agenda, with a smaller territorial outreach. In fact, racialization
and ethnicization are the commonest forms of cultural or identity
parlance in Canada. This is not only the case with "whites" or "the
English" but also with "others" after they spend some time in the
country. A language of colour, even self-appellations such as "women
of colour" (remember "coloured women"?), echo right through the
cultural/political world. An unofficial apartheid, of culture and
identity, organizes the social space of "Canada," first between whites
and non-whites, and then within the non-whites themselves.

A ROSE BY ANY OTHER NAME:
NAMING THE "OTHERS"

The transcendence or legitimation value of the official/state discourse of multiculturalism — which cherishes difference while erasing real antagonisms — breaks down, therefore, at different levels of competing ideologies and ruling practices. A threat of rupture or crisis is felt to be always already there, a fact expressed by the ubiquity of the integration-fragmentation paradigm in texts on Canada. Instead of a discourse of homogeneity or universality, the paradigm of multiculturalism stands more for the pressure of conflict of interests and dynamics of power relations at work. This language is useful for Canada since imagining a nation is a difficult task even when the society is more homogeneously based on historic and cultural sharing or hegemony. Issues of class, industry and capital constantly destabilize the national project even in its non-colonial context. Gramsci for example, in "Notes on Italian History," discusses the problem of unification inherent in the formation of a nation-state in the European bourgeois context (1971). Unificatory ideologies and institutions, emanating from the elite, posturing as a class-transcendent polity and implanted on top of a class society reveal as much as they hide. These attempts at unification forge an identifiable ideological core, a national identity, around which other cultural elements may be arranged hierarchically. It transpires that the ability and the right to interpret and name the nation's others forms a major task of national intellectuals, who are organic to the nation-state project.[20]

If this difficulty dogs European bourgeois nationalism, then it is a much more complicated task for Canada to imagine a *unificatory* national ideology, as recognized by members of the "white" ideological bloc espousing non-liberal perspectives. Ultra-conservatives in general have foresworn any pretence to the use of "multi-cultural" ideology. They view multiculturalism as an added burden to a society already divided, and accord no political or cultural importance to groups other than the French. The political grammar of "national" life and culture, as far as the near and far right are concerned, is common-sensically acknowledged as

"English." According importance to multiculturalism has the possibility of calling into question the "English" presence in this space, by creating an atmosphere of cultural relativism signalling some sort of usurpation. This signal, it is felt, is altogether best removed. English/Europeanness, that is, whiteness, emerges as the hegemonic Canadian identity. This white, Canadian and English equation becomes hegemonic enough to be shared even by progressive Canadians or the left.[21] This ideological Englishness/ whiteness is central to the programme of multiculturalism. It provides the content of Canadian culture, the point of departure for "multiculture." This same gesture creates "others" with power-organized "differences," and the material basis of this power lies both below and along the linguistic-semiotic level. Multiculturalism as the "other" of assimilation brings out the irreducible core of what is called the real Canadian culture.

So the meaning of Canada really depends on who is doing the imagining — whether it is Margaret Atwood or Charles Taylor or Northrop Frye or the "visible minorities" who organize conferences such as "Writing Thru 'Race.'" Depending on one's social location, the same snow and Canadian landscape, like Nellie McClung and other foremothers of Canadian feminism, can seem near or far, disturbing, threatening or benign. A search through the literature of the "visible minorities" reveals a terror of incarceration in the Canadian landscape.[22] In their Canada there is always winter and an equally cold and deathly cultural topography, filled with the RCMP, the Western Guard, the Heritage Front and the *Toronto Sun*, slain Native peoples and Sitting Bull in a circus tent, white-faced church fathers, trigger-happy impassive police, the flight and plight of illegals, and many other images of fear and active oppression. To integrate with this Canada would mean a futile attempt at integrating with a humiliation and an impossibility. Names of our otherness proliferate endlessly, weaving margins around "Canada/ English/French Canada." To speak of pan-Canadian nationalism and show a faith in "our" national institutions is only possible for those who can imagine it and already are "Canada." For "others," Canada can mean the actuality of skinhead attacks, the mediated fascism of the Reform Party, and the hard-fist of Rahowa.[23]

It is time to reflect on the nomenclature extended by multiculturalism to the "others" of "Canada." Its discourse is concocted through ruling relations and the practical administration of a supposed reconciliation of "difference." The term visible minorities is a great example: one is instantly struck by its reductive character, in which peoples from many histories, languages, cultures and politics are reduced to a distilled abstraction. Other appellations follow suit — immigrants, ethnics, new Canadians and so on. Functional, invested with a legal social status, these terms capture the "difference" from "Canada/English/French Canada" and often signify a newness of arrival into "Canada." Unlike a rose which by any other name, would smell as sweet, these names are not names in the sense of classification. They are in their inception and coding official categories. They are identifying devices, like a badge, and they identify those who hold no legitimate or possessive relationship to "Canada." Though these are often identity categories produced by the state, the role played by the state in identity politics remains unnoticed, just as the whiteness in the "self" of "Canada's" state and nationhood remains unnamed. This transparency or invisibility can only be achieved through a constellation of power relations that advances a particular group's identity as universal, as a measuring rod for others, making them "visible" and "minorities."

An expression such as visible minorities strikes the uninitiated as both absurd and abstract. "Minority," we know from J.S. Mill onwards, is a symptom of liberal democracy, but "visible?" We realize upon reflection that the adjective visible attached to minority makes the scope of identity and power even more restricted. We also know that it is mainly the Canadian state and politics which are instrumental in this categorizing process and confers this "visibility" upon us. I have remarked on its meaning and use elsewhere:

> Some people, it implies, are more visible than others; if this were not the case, then its triviality would make it useless as a descriptive category. There must be something "peculiar" about some people which draws attention to them. This something is the point to which the Canadian state wishes to draw our attention. Such a project of the state needed a point of departure

which has to function as a norm, as the social average of appearance. The well-blended, "average," "normal" way of looking becomes the base line, or "us" (which is the vantage point of the state), to which those others marked as "different" must be referred ... and in relation to which "peculiarity" [and thus, visibility] is constructed. The "invisibility" ... depends on the state's view of [some] as normal, and therefore, their institution as dominant types. They are true Canadians, and others, no matter what citizenship they hold [and how many generations have they lived here?] are to be considered as deviations.... (1993, p. 148)[24]

Such "visibility" indicates not only "difference" and inferiority, but is also a preamble to "special treatment." The yellow Star of David, the red star, the pink triangle, have all done their fair share in creating visibility along the same lines — if we care to remember. Everything that can be used is used as fodder for visibility, pinning cultural and political symbols to bodies and reading them in particular ways. Thus for non-whites in Canada,

their own bodies are used to construct for them some sort of social zone or prison, since they can not crawl out of their skins, and this signals what life has to offer them in Canada. This special type of visibility is a social construction as well as a political statement. (p. 149)

Expressions such as "ethnics" and "immigrants" and "new Canadians" are no less problematic. They also encode the "us" and "them" with regard to political and social claims, signifying uprootedness and the pressure of assimilation or core cultural-apprenticeship. The irony compounds when one discovers that all white people, no matter when they immigrate to Canada or as carriers of which European ethnicity, become invisible and hold a dual membership in Canada, while others remain immigrants generations later.

The issue of ethnicity, again, poses a further complexity. It becomes apparent that currently it is mainly applied to the non-white population living in Canada. Once, however, it stringently marked out white "others" to the Anglo-French language and ethos; while today the great "white" construction has assimilated them.

In the presence of contrasting "others," whiteness as an ideological-political category has superseded and subsumed different cultural ethos among Europeans. If the Ukrainians now seek to be ethnics it is because the price to be paid is no longer there. Now, in general, they are white *vis-à-vis* "others," as is denoted by the vigorous participation of East Europeans in white supremacist politics. They have been ingested by a "white-Anglo" ethos, which has left behind only the debris of self-consciously resurrected folklores as special effects in "ethnic" shows. The ethnicities of the English, the Scottish, the Irish, etc. are not visible or highlighted, but rather displaced by a general Englishness, which means less a particular culture than an official ideology and a standardized official language signifying the right to rule. "Ethnicity" is, therefore, what is classifiable as a non-dominant, sub or marginal culture. English language and Canadian culture then cannot fall within the ministry of multiculturalism's purview, but rather within that of the ministry of education, while racism makes sure that the possession of this language as a mother tongue does not make a non-white person non ethnic. Marginalizing the ethnicity of black people from the Caribbean or Britain is evident not only in the Caribana Festival but in their being forced to take English as a second language. They speak dialects, it is said — but it might be pointed out that the white Irish, the white Scots, or the white people from Yorkshire, or white Cockney speakers are not classified as ESL/ESD clients. The lack of fuss with which "Canadians" live with the current influx of Eastern European immigrants strikes a profound note of contrast to their approach to the Somalis, for example, and other "others."

The intimate relation between the Canadian state and racism also becomes apparent if one complements a discussion on multiculturalism with one on political economy. One could perhaps give a finer name than racism to the way the state organizes labour importation and segmentation of the labour market in Canada, but the basic point would remain the same. Capitalist development in Canada, its class formation and its struggles, predominantly have been organized by the Canadian state. From the days of indenture to the present, when the Ministry of "Manpower" has been transformed into that of "Human Resources," decisions about who should come into Canada to do what work, definitions of skill and accreditation, licensing and certification, have been influenced by "race" and ethnicity.[25] This type of racism cannot be grasped in its real character solely as a cultural/attitudinal problem or an issue of prejudice. It needs to be understood in systemic terms of political economy and the Gramscian concepts of hegemony and common sense that encompass all aspects of life — from the everyday and cultural ones to those of national institutions. This is apparent if one studies the state's role in the importation of domestic workers into Canada from the Philippines or the Caribbean. Makeda Silvera, in *Silenced*, her oral history of Caribbean domestic workers, shows the bonds of servitude imposed on these women by the state through the inherently racist laws pertaining to hiring of domestic workers.[26] The middle-man/procurer role played by the state on behalf of the "Canadian" bourgeoisie is glaringly evident. Joyce Fraser's *Cry of the Illegal Immigrant* is another testimonial to this (1980). The issue of refugees is another, where we can see the colonial/racist as well as anti-Communist nature of the Canadian state. Refugees fleeing ex-Soviet bloc countries, for example, received a no-questions acceptance, while the Vietnamese boat people, though fleeing communism, spent many years proving their claim of persecution. The racism of the state was so profound that even cold-war politics or general anti-communism did not make Vietnamese refugees into a "favoured" community. The story of racism is further exposed by the onerous and lengthy torture-proving rituals imposed on Latin Americans and others fleeing fascist dictatorships in the Third World. In spite of Canada's self-proclaimed commitment to human rights, numerous NGOs, both local and international, for years have needed to persuade the Canadian state and intervene as advocates of Third World refugees. Thus the state of "Canada," when viewed through the lens of racism/difference, presents us with a hegemony compounded of a racialized common sense and institutional structures. The situation is one where racism in all its cultural and institutional variants has become so naturalized, so pervasive that it has become invisible or transparent to those who are not adversely impacted by them. This is why terms such as visible minority can generate so spontaneously within the bureaucracy, and are not considered disturbing by most people acculturated to "Canada."

Erol Lawrence in his Gramscian critique "Plain Common Sense: The 'Roots' of Racism," (1986) uses the notion of common-sense racism to explain the relationship between the British blacks and the state. He displays how common sense of "race" marks every move of the state, including official nomenclatures and their implementation in social and political culture. Lawrence remarks on how hegemony works through common sense or expresses itself as such:

> The term common sense is generally used to denote a down-to-earth "good sense." It is thought to represent the distilled truths of centuries of practical experience; so much so that to say of an idea or practice that it is only common sense, is to appeal over the logic and argumentation of intellectuals to what all reasonable people know in their "heart of hearts" to be right and proper. Such an appeal can all at once and at the same time (serve) to foreclose any discussion about certain ideas and practices and to legitimate them. (1986, p. 48)

The point of this statement becomes clearer when we see how the Canadian state, the media and political parties are using "visible minorities," "immigrants," "refugees" and "illegals" as scapegoats for various economic and political problems entirely unrelated to them. For this they rely on common sense racism: they offer pseudo-explanations to justify crises of capitalism and erosion of public spending and social welfare in terms of the presence of "others." Unemployment, endemic to capital's "structural adjustment," is squarely blamed on "these people." This explanation/legitimation easily sticks because it replicates cultural-political values and practices that pre-exist on the ground. These labelling categories with racialized underpinnings spin-off into notions such as unskilled, illiterate and traditional, thus making the presence of Third World peoples undesirable and unworthy of real citizenship. Englishness and whiteness are the hidden positive poles of these degrading categories. They contain the imperative of exclusion and restriction that neatly fits the white supremacist demand to "keep Canada white." The multiculturalist stance may support a degree of tolerance, but beyond a certain point, on the far edge of equality, it asserts "Canadianness" and warns off "others" from making claims on "Canada." Through the same scale of values East European immigrants are seen as desirable because they can be included in the ideology of whiteness.

"Difference" read through "race," then, produces a threat of racist violence. The creation of a "minority" rather than of full-fledged adult citizens — the existence of levels of citizenship — adds a structural/legal dimension to this violence. Inequality within the social fabric of Canada historically has been strengthened by the creation of reserves, the Department of Indian Affairs, the exclusion of Jews, and the ongoing political inequalities meted out to the Chinese, the Japanese and South Asians. These and more add up to the tenuousness of the right and means to existence, jobs and politics of the "visible minorities." Being designated a minority signals tutelage. It creates at best a patron-client relationship between the state and "others" who are to be rewarded as children on the basis of "good conduct." Social behaviour historically created through class, "race" and gender oppression is blamed on the very people who have been the victims. Their problems are seen as self-constructed. The problem of crime in Toronto, for example, is mainly blamed on the black communities. Black young males are automatically labelled as criminals and frequently shot by the police. It is also characteristic that an individual act of violence performed by any black person is seen as a representative act for the whole black community, thus labelling them as criminal, while crime statistics among the white population remain non-representative of whiteness.

Visible minorities, because they are lesser or inauthentic political subjects, can enter politics mainly on the ground of multiculturalism. They can redress any social injustice only limitedly, if at all. No significant political effectiveness on a national scale is expected from them. This is why Elijah Harper's astute use of the tools of liberal democracy during the Meech Lake Accord was both unexpected and shocking for "Canadians." Other than administering "difference" differentially, among the "minority communities" multiculturalism bares the political processes of cooptation or interpellation. The "naming" of a political subject in an ideological context amounts to the creation of a political agent interpellating or extending an ideological net around her/him, which confers agency only within a certain discursive-political framework. At once minimizing the importance and administering the problem of racism at a symptomatic level, the notion of visible minority does not allow room for political manoeuvre among those for whose supposed benefit it is instituted. This is unavoidably accompanied by the ethnicization and communalization of politics, shifting the focus from unemployment due to high profit margins, or flight of capital, to "problems " presented by the immigrants own culture and tradition. Violence against women among the "ethnics" is thought to be the result of their indigenous "traditions" rather than of patriarchy and its exacerbation, caused by the absolute power entrusted by the Canadian state into the hands of the male "head of the family." The sponsorship system through which women and children enter into the country seems calculated to create violence. Food, clothes and so-called family values are continually centre-staged, while erasing the fundamental political and economic demands and aspirations of the communities through multicultural gestures of reconciling "difference." The agent of multiculturalism must learn to disarticulate from his or her real-life needs and struggles, and thus from creating or joining organizations for anti-racism, feminism and class struggle. The agencies (wo)manned by the "ethnic" elements — within terms and conditions of the state — become managers on behalf of the state. In fact, organizing multiculturalism among and by the non-white communities amounts to extending the state into their everyday life, and making basic social contradictions to disappear or be deflected. Considering the state's multicultural move therefore allows a look into the state's interpellative functions and how it works as an ideological apparatus. These administrative and ideological categories create *objects* out of the people they impact upon and produce mainstream agencies in their name. In this way a little niche is created within the state for those who are otherwise undesirable, unassimilable and deeply different. Whole communities have begun to be re-named on the basis of these conferred cultural administrative identities that objectify and divide them. Unrelated to each other, they become clients and creatures of the multicultural state. Entire areas of problems connected to "race," class, gender and sexual orientation are brought under the state's management, definition and control, and possibilities for the construction of political struggles are displaced and erased in the name of "ethnic culture." The politics of identity among "ethnic communities," that so distresses the "whites" and is seen as an excessive permissiveness on the part of the state, is in no small measure the creation of this very culturalist managerial/legitimation drive of the state.

What, then, is to be done? Are we to join forces with the Reform Party or the small "c" conservative "Canadians" and advocate that the agenda of multiculturalism be dropped summarily? Should we be hoping for a deeper legitimation crisis through unemployment and rampant cultural racism, which may bring down the state? In theory that is an option, except that in the current political situation it also would strengthen the ultra-right. But strategically speaking, at this stage of Canadian politics, with the withdrawal and disarray of the left and an extremely vulnerable labour force, the answer can not be so categorical. The political potential of the civil society even when (mis)named as ethnic communities and reshaped by multiculturalism is not a negligible force. This view is validated by the fact that all shades of the right are uneasy with multiculturalism even though it is a co-opted form of popular, non-white political and cultural participation. The official, limited and co-optative nature of this discourse could be re-interpreted in more materialist historical and political terms. It could then be re-articulated to the social relations of power governing our lives, thus minimizing, or even ending, our derivative, peripheral object agent status. The basic nature of our "difference," as constructed in the Canadian context, must be rethought and the notion of culture once more embedded into society, into everyday life. Nor need it be forgotten that what multiculturalism (as with social welfare) gives us was not "given" voluntarily but "taken" by our continual demands and struggles. We must remember that it is our own socio-cultural and economic resources which are thus minimally publicly redistributed, creating in the process a major legitimation gesture for the state. Multiculturalism as a form of bounty or state patronage is a managed version of our antiracist politics.

We must then bite the hand that feeds us, because what it feeds us is neither enough nor for our good. But we must wage a contestation on this terrain with the state and the needs of a racist/ imperialist capital. At this point of the new world order, short of risking an out-and-out fascism, the twisted ideological evolution of multiculturalism has to be forced into a minimum scope of social politics. Until we have developed a wider political space, and perhaps with it keeping a balance of "difference," using the avenues of liberal democracy may be necessary. Informed with a critique, multiculturalism is a small opening for making the state minimally accountable to those on whose lives and labour it erects itself. We must also remember that liberalism, no matter who practises it, does not answer our real needs. Real social relations of power — of "race," class, gender and sexuality — provide the content for our "difference" and oppression. Our problem is not the value or the validity of the cultures in which we or our parents originated — these "home" cultures will, as living cultures do in history, undergo a sea-change when subjected to migration. Our problem is class oppression, and that of objectifying sexist-racism. Thinking in terms of culture alone, in terms of a single community, a single issue, or a single oppression will not do. If we do so our ideological servitude to the state and its patronage and funding traps will never end. Instead we need to put together a strategy of articulation that reverses the direction of our political understanding and affiliation — against the interpellating strategies of the ideological state apparatus. We need not forget that the very same social relations that disempower or minoritize us are present not only for us but in the very bones of class formation and oppression in Canada. They are not only devices for cultural discrimination and attitudinal distortion of the white population, or only a mode of co-optation for "visible minorities." They show themselves inscribed into the very formation of the nation and the state of "Canada." Thus the politics of class struggle, of struggle against poverty or heterosexism or violence against women, are politically more relevant for us than being elected into the labyrinth of the state. The "visible minorities" of Canada can not attain political adulthood and full stature of citizenship without struggling, both conceptually and organizationally, against the icons and regulations of an overall subordination and exploitation.

In conclusion, then, to answer the questions "How are we to relate to multiculturalism?" and "Are we for it or against it?" we have to come to an Aesopian response of "ye, ye" and "nay, nay."

After all, multiculturalism, as Marx said of capital, is not a "thing." It is not a cultural object, all inert, waiting on the shelf to be bought or not. It is a mode of the workings of the state, an expression of an interaction of social relations in dynamic tension with each other, losing and gaining its political form with fluidity. It is thus a site for struggle, as is "Canada" for contestation, for a kind of tug-of war of social forces. The problem is that no matter who we are — black or white — our liberal acculturation and single-issue oriented politics, our hegemonic "subsumption" into a racist common sense, combined with capital's crisis, continually draw us into the belly of the beast. This can only be prevented by creating counter-hegemonic interpretive and organizational frame-works that reach down into the real histories and relations of our social life, rather than extending tendrils of upward mobility on the concrete walls of the state. Our politics must sidestep the paradigm of "unity" based on "fragmentation or integration" and instead engage in struggles based on the genuine contradictions of our society.

NOTES

1   This division of Canada into Quebec and Canada outside of Quebec (COQ) is used as more than a territorial expression by Taylor (1993).

2   For an exposition of the notions of "solitude" and "survival," see Atwood (1972).

3   For an elaboration of these concepts, see Althusser (1977).

4   On multiculturalism, its definition and history, see Fleras and Elliot (1992).

5   On the emergence of a liberal state from the basis of a white settler colony, see Bolaria and Li (1988). Also see Kulchyski (1994) and Tester and Kulchyski (1994). For a "race"/gender inscription into a semi-colonial Canadian state, see Monture-Angus (1995).

6   For an in-depth discussion of mediatory and unificatory ideologies needed by a liberal democratic, i.e. capitalist state, see Miliband (1984) chs. 7 & 8.

7   For a clarification of my use of this concept, see Habermas (1975). This use of "legitimacy" is different from Charles Taylor's Weberian use of it in *Reconciling the Solitudes* (1993).

8   See Anderson (1991), Introduction and ch. 2. Anderson says, "I...propose the following definition of the nation: it is an imagined political community — and imagined as both inherently limited and sovereign. It is *imagined* because

the members of even the smallest nation will never know most of their fellow members, meet them, or even hear of them, yet in the minds of each lives the image of their communion" (p. 6).

9   In *Reconciling* (ch. 4) on "Alternative Futures" for Canada, Taylor fleshes out his desirable and undesirable options for Canada. This is also found in his *Multiculturalism and "the Politics of Recognition"* (1992).

10 Taylor is quite direct about his German romantic intellectual heritage. In *Reconciling*, in an essay entitled "Institutions in National Life," he states, "In Herder I found inspiration, ideas that were very fruitful for me, precisely because I was from here, I was able to understand him from the situation I had experienced outside school, outside university, and I was able to engage with his thought, internalize it, and (I hope) make something interesting out of it" (p. 136).

11 For an exposition of this idea, and Taylor's rejection of an "American" solution for "Canadian" identity, see "Shared and Divergent" in *Reconciling*.

12 On the development of active white supremacist groups in Canada, and their "Englishness," see Robb (1992). Also Ward (1978).

13 But see also the chapter on "Official Nationalism and Imperialism" (Anderson, 1991).

14 On the construction of "whiteness" as an ideological, political and socio-historical category see Allen (1994), and Roediger (1993); also Frankenberg (1993).

15 On the use of "whiteness"/Europeanness as an ideology for ruling, including its formative impact on sexuality of the ruling, colonial nations, see Stoller (1995).

16 On this theme see Joseph Conrad's *The Heart of Darkness*, E.M. Forster's *A Passage to India* and Said (1993).

17 On the reading of the black, dark or "visible minority" body, see the collection of essays in Gates (1985), especially Gillman, "Black Bodies, White Bodies."

18 See Stoller (1995), but also Sinha (1995).

19 The history of immigration and refugee laws in Canada, and of the immigrants, indentured workers and refugees themselves, must be read to comprehend fully what I am attempting to say. See The Law Union of Ontario (1981). Also Canada (1974), and Canada (1986).

20 On organic intellectuals as intellectuals who are integral to any ideological and class project, see Gramsci, "The Intellectuals," in Gramsci (1971).

21 This becomes evident when we follow the controversies which are generated by writers' conferences, such as "Writing thru Race," or the black communities' response and resistance to the Royal Ontario Museum's exhibition on African art and culture, "Out of the Heart of Africa."

22 See, for example, Brand (1983), Sri Bhaggiyadatta (1993), H. Bannerji (1986), and collections such as McGifford and Kearn (1990).

23 The acronym for Racial Holy War, a neo-nazi rock band.

24 On this theme of social construction of a racialized "minority" subject and its inherent patriarchy, see Carty and Brand (1993) and Ng (1993).

25 See Avery (1995). Much work still needs to be done in this area, in which class formation is considered in terms of both "race" and gender, but a beginning is made in Brand (1991), and Brand and Sri Bhaggiyadatta (1985).

26 This is powerfully brought forth through the issue of the importation of domestic workers to Toronto from the Caribbean in Silvera (1989).

REFERENCES

Allen, Theodor. *The Invention of the White Race: Racial Oppression and Social Control.* London: Verso, 1994.

Althusser, Louis. "Ideology and Ideological State Apparatuses (Notes towards an Investigation)." In *Lenin and Philosophy and Other Essays.* London: New Left Books, 1977.

Anderson, Benedict. *Imagined Communities.* London: Verso, 1991.

Atwood, Margaret. *Survival: A Thematic Guide to Canadian Literature.* Toronto: House of Anansi Press, 1972.

Avery, Donald. *Reluctant Host: Canada's Response to Immigrant Workers, 1896-1994.* Toronto: McClelland & Stewart, 1995.

Bannerji, Himani. *Doing Time.* Toronto: Sister Vision Press, 1986.

———. "Images of South Asian Women." In *Returning the Gaze: Essays on Racism, Feminism and Politics.* Ed. Himani Bannerji. Toronto: Sister Vision Press, 1993.

———, ed. *Returning the Gaze: Essays on Racism, Feminism and Politics.* Toronto: Sister Vision Press, 1993.

Bannerji, Kaushalya. *A New Remembrance.* Toronto: TSAR Publications, 1993.

Bolaria, B. Singh, and Peter Li, eds. *Racial Oppression in Canada.* Toronto: Garamond Press, 1988.

Brand, Dionne. *Winter Epigrams.* Toronto: Williams-Wallace, 1983.

———. *No Burden to Carry: Narratives of Black Working Women in Ontario, 1920s to 1950s.* Toronto: Women's Press, 1991.

Brand, Dionne, and Krisantha Sri Bhaggiyadatta, eds. *Rivers Have Sources, Trees Have Roots: Speaking of Racism.* Toronto: Cross Cultural Communications Centre, 1985.

Canada. Department of Manpower and Immigration and Information. *A Report of the Canadian Immigration and Population Study: Immigration Policy Perspective.* Ottawa: Queen's Printer, 1974.

Canada. House of Commons. *Equality Now: Report of the Special Committee on Visible Minorities.* Ottawa: Queen's Printer, 1986.

Carty, Linda, and Dionne Brand. "Visible Minority Women: A Creation of the Colonial State." In *Returning the Gaze: Essays on Racism, Feminism and Politics.* Ed. Himani Bannerji. Toronto: Sister Vision Press, 1993.

Fleras, Angie, and Jean Leonard Elliot, eds. *Multiculturalism in Canada: The Challenge of Diversity.* Scarborough: Nelson, 1992.

Frankenberg, Ruth. *White Women, Race Matters: The Social Construction of Whiteness.* Minneapolis: University of Minnesota Press, 1993.

Fraser, Joyce. *Cry of the Illegal Immigrant.* Toronto: Williams-Wallace Productions International, 1980.

Gates Jr., Henry Louis, ed. *"Race," Writing and Difference.* Chicago: The University of Chicago Press, 1985.

Gillman, Sander. "Black Bodies, White Bodies." In *"Race," Writing and Difference.* Ed. Henry Louis Gates Jr. Chicago: The University of Chicago Press, 1985.

Gramsci, Antonio. *Selections from the Prison Notebooks,* edited and translated by Quentin Hoare and Geoffrey Smith. New York: International Publishers, 1971.

Habermas, Jurgen. *Legitimation Crisis.* Boston: Beacon Press, 1975.

Kulchyski, Peter, ed. *Unjust Relations: Aboriginal Rights in Canadian Courts.* Toronto: Oxford University Press, 1994.

Law Union of Ontario, The. *The Immigrant's Handbook.* Montreal: Black Rose Books. 1981.

Lawrence, Erol. "Just Plain Common Sense: The 'Roots' of Racism," in *The Empire Strikes Back: Race and Racism in 70s Britain.* London: Centre for Contemporary Cultural Studies, Hutchinson, in association with the Centre for Cultural Studies, University of Birmingham, 1986.

McGifford, Diane, and Judith Kearn, eds. *Shakti's Words.* Toronto: TSAR, 1990.

Miliband, Ralph. *The State in Capitalist Society.* London: Quartet Books, 1984.

Monture-Angus, Patricia. *Thunder in My Soul: A Mohawk Woman Speaks.* Halifax: Fernwood, 1995.

Ng, Roxana. "Sexism, Racism, Canadian Nationalism." In *Returning the Gaze: Essays on Racism, Feminism and Politics.* Ed. Himani Bannerji. Toronto: Sister Vision Press, 1993.

Robb, Martin. *Shades of Right: Nativist and Fascist Politics in Canada, 1920-1940.* Toronto: University of Toronto Press, 1992.

Roediger, David. *The Wages of Whiteness: Race and the Making of the American Working Class*. London: Verso, 1993.

Said, Edward. *Culture and Imperialism*. New York: Vintage Books, 1993.

Silvera, Makeda. *Silenced: Talks With Working Class Caribbean Women about Their Lives and Struggles as Domestic Workers in Canada*, 2nd edition. Toronto: Sister Vision Press, 1989.

Sinha, Mrinalini. *Colonial Masculinity*. Manchester: Manchester University Press, 1995.

Sri Bhaggiyadatta, Krisantha. *Domestic Bliss*. Toronto: Five Press, 1981.

———. *The 52nd State of Amnesia*. Toronto: TSAR, 1993.

Stoller, Ann Laura. *Race and the Education of Desire: Foulcault's History of Sexuality and the Colonial Order of Things*. Durham: Duke University Press, 1995.

Taylor, Charles. *Multiculturalism and "the Politics of Recognition."* Princeton: Princeton University Press, 1992.

———. *Reconciling the Solitudes: Essays on Canadian Federalism and Nationalism*. Ed. Guy Laforest. Montreal and Kingston: McGill-Queen's University Press, 1993.

Tester, Frank, and Peter Kulchyski, *Tammarniit (Mistakes): Relocation in the Eastern Arctic*. Vancouver: University of British Columbia Press, 1994.

Ward, William Peter. *White Canada Forever*. Montreal: McGill-Queen's University Press, 1978.

CHAPTER 4

Charles Taylor's
Politics of Recognition:
A Critique

*P*itfalls of political consciousness associated with multiculturalism should not prevent us from realizing that its meaning is context specific. Meaning and application of multiculturalism vary depending on who initiates it, on what theoretical and practical grounds, and why. Judging from this point of view, what I have called "multiculturalism from above" ceases to be only an official category, an aspect of the ideological apparatus of the state. We find another version of it in the work of intellectuals, whom Gramsci (1974) would call "organic intellectuals" of bourgeois society, who, from their elite standpoint as "traditional intellectuals" elaborate supportive theories. Though these intellectuals refuse state intervention in cultural and moral matters, preferring instead to create a situation of adjudication by philosophers and experts, they nonetheless reason in such a way that the prevalent organization of ruling relations and ideologies are not only not disturbed, but actually reaffirmed. In Charles Taylor we find such an elite organic intellectual of Canada, who in his essay "The Politics of Recognition" (1994) makes a philosophical intervention or attempt at arbitration in what he sees as a nasty squabble over cultural rights. Taylor's approach, which differentiates itself from the Canadian state's official multicultural policy and speaks from communitarian grounds, is an excellent example of non-official elite multiculturalism.

Although the works of Charles Taylor, and "The Politics of Recognition" in particular, have been widely read and generally admired, his position on cultural politics, variously named as "politics of difference," "politics of representation" and "politics of cultural rights," has not been sufficiently explored or critiqued. The responses have been generally framed within a narrow and binary theoretical parameter of communitarianism versus individual rights, or romantic conservatism versus liberalism. In the Canadian context these two positions are represented by Charles Taylor and Will Kymlicka, respectively. But there is a need to go beyond this simplistic perception and a state versus community position, to see if these two seemingly antithetical positions do not share a common ground, and also if it is not possible to adopt a third theoretical and political position from which both of these can be critiqued. This present critical exploration of "The Politics of Recognition" is conducted from that third position — that of antiracist and marxist feminism.

This critique of a single essay, though conducted with a general knowledge of Taylor's other works of social philosophy, is avowedly limited. It is the initial sketch of a larger project, and meant not just as a response to Taylor, but rather as a way of creating a critical space beyond the paradigms of liberal and conservative thought. It refuses the separation that they postulate between forms of thought or political and cultural consciousness and social and historical relations elaborated by local and extra-local political-economic organizations. In other words, it is a critical reading conducted from a historical materialist position, particularly reliant upon the critique of ideology offered by Marx and Engels (1973) in *The German Ideology*. It views the emergence of multiculturalism as a ruling category and its treatment in both the official and elite form as ideological. To this marxist view of ideology as a "relation of ruling" (Smith, 1987) it adds Gramsci's concept of hegemony as a way of connecting social or class power to cultural common sense and daily practices. It is from this critical vantage point that it claims Charles Taylor's understanding of the relationship between culture and society or political power as being ideological and augmenting of the existing elite anglo-European hegemony in Canada.

Considered from my critical epistemological standpoint, Taylor is a more complex thinker than conventional liberals. He is not so much in opposition to liberal thought and the gains of modernity as he is in a mood for their modification. He is a good citizen of the liberal state, doing his part in enriching the liberal social ethos by drawing upon aspects of European conservative and romantic as well as christian thought.

"The Politics of Recognition" has been much discussed and admired by academics and community activists around the world. The world of "multicultural education" in Canada resounds with this phrase and sees it as an empowering tool. To such people this critique will no doubt come as a surprise. And it is not hard to see why those who want to retain a cultural sensitivity, care for issues of identity and a holistic approach to social life would be drawn to Charles Taylor, rather than to a rationalist accounting of individual rights and the maximization of utilities as promulgated by liberal thought or the state. The reflective tone of Charles Taylor's writings on self and society (Taylor, 1989), his constant reference to a collective "we," his cognizance of feelings, imagination, cultural identity and difference, are generally more appealing than an abstract and individualistic liberalism, which C. B. Macpherson (1977) has shown to be a legacy of Benthamite Utilitarianism. Amy Gutmannn's (1994) collection of responses to Taylor's essay, "The Politics of Recognition," by renowned philosophers and political theorists is a tribute to his contribution in attempting to offer a solution to the malaise of modernity. But all of this does not take away from the fact that the debate on multiculturalism needs to move beyond the simplicity of choices between liberalism and quasi-liberal and conservative communitarianism, allowing for other positions of collectivity, such as the one attempted by this critique.

A close reading of Taylor's "The Politics of Recognition" shows that he can not be simply posed as a communitarian conservative to liberalism's concept of individual rights, or as someone who denies entirely the validity of a liberal state. This polarization does not hold, in spite of Taylor's anti-Kantian stance, his awareness of the shortcomings of modernity and his great scholarship of Hegel. He does not attempt a full retreat from modernity, though he speaks openly of his attachment to romantic and organicist philosophers such as Herder,[1] or of his indebtedness to Hegel (Taylor, 1979). He is very much with us, in the Canada of here and now, participating in political debates and discussions which range from Quebec's secession to globalization and its impact on Canada as well as on multiculturalism and Canadian society. He has sought to make a contribution to what is called "identity politics" by offering a pragmatic solution which modifies tenets of liberalism or modernity in order to ultimately save it.[2] His writings, from this point of view, may be seen as the erection of a communitarian fortification around the current core of liberal democracy and the (Canadian) state. It is important to note that he has done this by means of infusing aspects of conservative thought into the liberal world in order to add to a modern society and the liberal state elements of collectivity and invention of tradition. Taylor cannot be seen as a classically conservative figure, but rather as a conservative liberal.

The hallmark of Taylor's affinity with conservatives or romantic philosophers lies in his sensitivity to alienation and individualism produced by an industrial society with its technological, utilitarian rationality, social atomism, moral apathy and a cost accountancy of pleasure. The difference is that Taylor is not in a mood for their thoroughgoing denunciation, but rather wishes to preserve some aspects of modernity and liberal democracy while accommodating or conserving some older European values or traditions. In short, he wishes to retain an older European cultural identity in the face of what he considers to be a mass culture and an exaggerated egalitarianism.[3] Both in his tone and in the formulation of his concerns Taylor reminds us of anglo-catholic philosophers and social critics such as Coleridge, T. H. Greene and T. S. Eliot. In the Canadian context George Grant or Northrop Frye may also come to mind. Like these social thinkers, Taylor does not take into account the history, social relations and politics that lead to or accompany the technological development and its deployment. Thus issues of capital, class, ideology and imperialism are of no relevance in his social philosophy. Instead he slips from a particular social situation into a metaphysics of the human condition, thus cutting off forms of consciousness from their social ground and obscuring history. It is through this metaphysical gesture that Taylor's world view acquires a holistic character, because otherwise the separation which he assumes between the different moments of the social, such as between the political, the cultural and the economic, would identify him as a practitioner of liberal thought.

In "The Politics of Recognition" Taylor looks at the pre-modern past of Europe and contrasts it with the modern and the post-modern times in terms of a change in mentality, a movement from days of a collective, cohesive community with a common christian moral world view, to those of an abstract equality between individuals.[4] This earlier unfractured moral universe is one of an invention of tradition, a construction that is tinted with nostalgia, but it is also realistically relinquished as mostly lost. Aspects of it are sought to be reinvented or recuperated in our liberal times. The development of modernist notions of social equality and individual rights and the formation of a liberal state break the links in a great chain of Being, with its graduated social order. This order, Taylor reminds us, is based on a sense of difference rather than a demand for equality, and it is linked to social deference and a system of preference or honour. It is this feudal, organic, christian European community which disappears when the liberal/modernist demand for equality ushers in a new social and political era. It aims at a kind of levelling, of an elimination of socially accepted forms of difference, deference and preference, which ultimately produces a sense of alienation and conflict, the malaise of modernity. This transition from the feudal pre-modern to the modern liberal phase is sketched by Taylor as a progression from ideas to ideas. Forms of consciousness overdetermining the socio-temporal succeed each other in stages. This movement obscures their historically contingent nature, as well as the social contradictions and struggles which marked their emergence, continuity and disappearance. Thus viewed from the standpoint of history of ideas, struggle for hegemony and human condition become indistinguishable from each other.

This pseudo-history is further presented by Taylor in two stages of the development of liberal thought.[5] As he sees it, liberalism in its first Kantian phase creates a politics of equality by suppressing difference through a universalist abstraction. It creates a politics of abstract equality, of equal rights, as though each individual were the same as the other. Critically and correctly emphasizing the fictive nature of this equality, and that of the persona of the individual, Taylor omits to criticize the equally constructed socially dominant, power organized nature of a social order of difference in pre-feudal times. He seems not to mind that the older notion of difference was neither a matter of culture or of personal characteristics, but rather one of a feudal order of subordination, which he himself signals by speaking of deference, preference and honour. But he goes on to note that this abstract universality of liberalism, with its democracy of abstract individual equality and rights, enters into its present phase by now seeking to incorporate cultural difference into the procedural apparatus of the state, by treating it as a part of the package of citizenship. This liberal politics, now extending to incorporate difference, is guilty of introjecting the notion of (individual) rights into the cultural realm, which amounts to a demand for an equality of difference by advocating an equal value or worth of all cultures.

This expansion of the liberal state into the cultural realm, that is, the elaboration of an official multiculturalism, is considered by Taylor to be illegitimate as it seeks to combine arguments of political equality with that of (cultural) difference. The required universalist abstraction for a liberal polity cannot cohere with the concreteness, the specificity of difference embodied by diverse social cultures. The liberal state's advocacy of multiculturalism is an act of contradiction, of having one's cake and eating it too. For if only by abstracting from difference (for example class, "race," gender, sexuality and so on) could liberal thought arrive at the persona of the rights-bearing equal individual or the citizen, then it could not appeal any more to the principle or actuality of difference among individuals to now create another sphere of rights. Taylor makes a succinct statement about this:

> Now underlying the demand is a principle of universal equality. The politics of difference is full of denunciations of discrimination and refusals of second-class citizenship. This gives the principle of universal equality a point of entry within the politics of dignity. But once inside, as it were, its demands are hard to assimilate to that politics. For it asks that we give acknowledgment and status to something that is not universally shared. Or, otherwise put, we give due acknowledgment only to what is universally present —

everyone has an identity — through recognizing what is peculiar to each. The universal demand powers an acknowledgment of specificity. (Taylor, 1994: 39)

Official multiculturalism thus disturbs Taylor both morally and philosophically because of its simultaneous demand for equality and difference, for its reliance on a universalist argument to validate the particular. As he sees it, political citizenship or an equality argument cannot be made into the basis for a cultural one as well. In order to illustrate his objection Taylor picks up from Saul Bellow's infamous remark on the Zulus who have yet to produce their Tolstoy.

> When Saul Bellow is famously quoted as saying something like, "When the Zulus produce a Tolstoy we will read him," this is taken as a quintessential statement of European arrogance, not just because Bellow is allegedly being *de facto* insensitive to the value of Zulu culture, but frequently also because it is seen to reflect a denial in principle of human equality. The possibility that the Zulus, while having the same potential for culture formation as anyone else, might nevertheless have come up with a culture that is less valuable than others is ruled out from the start. Even to entertain this possibility is to deny human equality. Bellow's error here, then, would not be a (possibly insensitive) particular mistake in evaluation, but a denial of a fundamental principle. (42)

According to Taylor, who ignores Bellow's racism, if Zulus can claim universal equality with Europeans as individuals only by being abstracted from their cultural particularity which makes them unable to produce a Tolstoy, then we cannot use an argument of equality to support a claim for the equality of their cultural difference. Europeans, we can see, do not need such arguments of equality to be equal to the Zulus.

From an antiracist feminist marxist position Taylor's use of difference as only a cultural category, uninscribed with relations of power, seems problematic. He seems not to make any distinction between different kinds of differences, those which could be called cultural diversities and those structured through power relations and which could be encoded as gender, "race" and class (Bannerji, 1995). Thus his criticism of difference-blind liberals who now claim difference into their equality argument further extends to a category of radical philosophers and critics who connect difference to representational and discursive forms of power. To connect culture with politics, he says angrily, is a half-baked neo-Nietzscheanism. This passage captures a crucial aspect of Taylor's argument against politics of representation connected to power/difference.

> In fact, subjectivist, half-baked neo-Nietzschean theories are quite often invoked in this debate. Deriving frequently from Foucault or Derrida, they claim that all judgements of worth are based on standards that are ultimately imposed by and further entrench structures of power. It should be clear why these theories proliferate here. A favorable judgement on demand is nonsense, unless some such theories are valid. (70)

If the proponents of power/knowledge with their discourses of difference are reprehensible to Taylor, marxists with their notions of ideology, class consciousness and class struggle are even more so, as they are unable to think of culture as independent of class and ideology, and thus incapable of having any understanding of difference.[6] The Gramscian concept of hegemony, implying a daily common sense sort of cultural domination which marks a certain type of difference, is also absent in Taylor's consideration. Instead his idea of difference involves a combination of an aesthetic resting in a sort of cultural genetics — as a phenomenon of ontology and taste. This is why Taylor can refuse to inquire into the reasons for the current emergence of the *politics of difference or representation*, as evidenced by his angry dismissal of antiracist and anti-oppression pedagogy and curriculum or his resistance to affirmative action (1994: 65-66). These he connects with a peculiar move to a procedural or official multiculturalism, a deformation introduced by the liberal state, as well as with Frantz Fanon, whom he misrepresents as an Afro-centric thinker of politics of recognition (65).

Because Taylor sees culture as separated from social relations, and discourses of power and difference as a sort of cultural diversity, and also lacks any theory of ideology or hegemony, he cannot see his own implication in the politics of difference. His ideological position and knowledge location are obscure to him, submerged as they are in his philosophical or metaphysical persona. By the same token he cannot identify what he considers as normal western culture as a hegemonic form of anglo-European culture. He attributes its national and international dominance to its intrinsic worth, to its civilizational superiority. The ghosts of Tolstoy and the Zulus haunt this civilizational rhetoric. So, of course, he can neither support state initiated or procedural multiculturalism nor any form of cultural politics of resistance. His very epistemology, his theoretical formulation, prevents that.

Though he complains about contradictions of official multiculturalism, a close reading of "The Politics of Recognition" shows a basic contradiction in Taylor's moral philosophy of multiculturalism. It is that of the upholding of a hegemonic particular — "European civilization" — while aspiring to a universal, metaphysical stance, a transcendence disciplinarily mandated to philosophers. This contradiction, which has political implications when applied to actual social relations, is largely masked by his holism and a tone of sweet reasonableness. It is also unnoticed by his commentators in the volume compiled by Amy Gutmann because they themselves lack a critical ground other than those of liberalism or conservatism. But it is also true that Taylor's smooth stylistics make it difficult to challenge his ideas for fear of appearing to be rude, of making a scene. But a large part of our critical enquiry lies in this very stylistics in order to find clues which explain a sense of unease experienced by some readers with this text. It is a kind of smothering hush that can befall someone in churches and museums. His concerned courteousness makes it a trifle difficult to call his Eurocentrism racism, or to point out how politically and personally oppressive it is for Canada's "others," such as non-white peoples, feminists, antiracists and gays and lesbians. But criticism requires that this seamless and flowing text which moves over us so conversationally be interrupted. We will have to take apart the dialogism of this text itself, which projects his sentiment of voluntary recognition in its written textual version. This will allow us to see how his text organizes and expresses social relations of power, albeit from within the civil society and a class position, from within the Platonic tradition of the philosopher guide of Canada's national project — both far from and near to the official multiculturalism of the Canadian state.

Charles Taylor sees the human condition as being dialogical in that identities are formed in relation to, in conversation with, others. It would then make sense to study the kind of dialogue he constructs in connection with identity and recognition. We begin, therefore, from the position that the dialogical organization of "The Politics of Recognition" mirrors the type of social dialogue expressed by Taylor's concept of "recognition." The text is meant to organize the position of the author and the reader, as well as the author's object of discussion. This organization is conducted by reference to general conditions of identity formation shown through the various deployments of the pronouns "we" and "they" and occasionally by "I." About the use of "we," a few variations should be noted. Sometimes it is an authorial "we," a plural used by authors to establish themselves within an intellectual tradition from where significant pronouncements can be made about a given topic. Sometimes Taylor uses another kind of "we" which expresses the universalist aspirations common to philosophers, drawing us together in a general human condition, as for example in such assertions as "[w]e define our identity always in dialogue with, sometimes in arguments against, the things our significant others want to see in us." (32-33) This also allows the author to establish general propositions or founding premises from which particular deductions can be made. Speaking in terms of a social dialogue, this "we" extends a gesture of communitarian hospitality — creates a space where the readers can come in if they feel themselves to be a part of this "we." But this is where a trouble arises when some readers, unable to claim an insider's status of the culture that Taylor sees as "our" culture, fall into the category of "they" about whose multiculture Taylor talks about.

At this point we have to recognize a "we" which is social and contingent in nature, a "we" that splits off into "us" (culture and people similar to Taylor) and "them." This "they" of Taylor may be the "we" of many, but is positioned in this text as a category of difference from Taylor's "us." Now the initial ground of universality, of common human condition, disappears, making it quite apparent that Taylor is writing from a particular socio-cultural location, considering some cultures to be "culture" while other, different cultures are components of multicultures. Immediately these others, "they," are put in an observed position, and in the position of the object of discussion. "They" overhear Taylor's discussions and debates with an "us" regarding both the need and ground for recognition of "their" multicultures and the extent to which this recognition should be accorded. The central questions for Taylor are: do "we" have any obligation to recognize "them," and do "they" have any right to force this recognition from "us"? These are the questions with which Taylor enters his problematic — the politics of recognition — or the contestation that is going on in Canada and other western countries regarding the affirmation and assertion of cultures which are different from anglo-European high culture. Taylor sees "their" politics of representation as a challenge to "our" politics of recognition.

Seen from this point of view of the impossibility of establishing a dialogue among equals, it becomes evident that, the tone of hospitality notwithstanding, the element of mutuality that is signalled by the philosophical level and necessary for a real situation of recognition is absent from Taylor's development of its premises and practicalities. An element of power is not only present in "their" demand for recognition, but in "our" terms and conditions for participating in it. In fact in the way the "us" and "them" situation asserts throughout the text the issue of multiculturalism gets directly and unidirectionally politicized. The reader realizes that the text is speaking of an anglo-European, so-called Canadian "us," who are being attributed the power of recognizing or not recognizing "them." But this dimension of power relations in constituting "our" and "their" cultural relations is sometimes obfuscated by slippages from this particular social "we" of Canadian national culture to the philosophical universal "we" to which Taylor appeals in order to bring about a non-political solution to the question of recognition. As he sees it, neither official multiculturalism nor the politics of representation can bring about the desired solution to the problem caused by the presence of ethnic/ cultural others in Canada or the West. Though he supports everyone's need for recognition and appeals to "us" who are in a position to grant it, he does not question why "we" have this power to grant or withhold it. He does not ask whether his discourse of recognition has moved from its universalist ground because it rests in the actuality of socio-historical relations of white settler colonies or former colonial powers still locked in imperialist relations to the rest of the world. After all, the very need for recognition of some by others signals to relations of power and ties cultural recognition to power/knowledge.

It is not that Taylor is unaware of this "us" and "them" relation. "The Politics of Recognition" or *Reconciling Solitudes* both signal to actualities existing between the anglo "us" and Quebec's others, or anglo "us" and multicultural others, which snap the bond of human condition. But he makes the others responsible for initiating the struggle for recognition, for pushing this basic "human" need into the realm of politics by constantly speaking of rights, by using the machinery of liberal democracy to force the recognition from "us." Worse still, "they" are combining it with a "half-baked neo-Nietzschean" — that is, Foucaultian or Derridian — politics, converting culture into a matter of hegemony. He refuses to recognize the political nature of the very situation where some cultures are non-adjectivally self-centred as Canadian or national culture, while others are designated ethnicities or multicultures.

But what becomes apparent to Taylor's readers, perhaps even those who are not on the receiving end of recognition, is that hegemony is signified by the very ease with which elite anglo-European culture can function as "culture" and can, therefore, claim universality and transcendence, while those of non-European others are particularized. Taylor is willing to entertain some pleas from "them" and tells his "us" that "we should do unto others as we would have done unto us." But under no condition can he endure an insistence on an intrinsic merit of "their" cultures or the flaunting of their difference from "our" cultures. This attitude on Taylor's part becomes evident when he speaks about the worth of "their" ragas in comparison with "our" well-tempered clavier composition by Bach (67).

In spite of his desire to play a philosophical role to arbitrate between contending parties and to keep culture and civil society from being annexed by the state, Taylor cannot avoid speaking from his ideologically occluded class position and in support of an anglo-European elite hegemony. His claim of a "philosophical" stance is contradicted or betrayed by the very tone of his narrative, which is driven by a sense of cultural crisis that is not simply a crisis or malaise of modernity, a perennial liberal dilemma. Rather it is created by a fear of being swamped by alien cultures. There is virtually a tone of panic when he reminds "us" that our borders are "porous," allowing in religions such as islam which plunge us into dilemmas of whether "we" should refuse "their" cultures.

> ... all societies are becoming increasingly multicultural, while at the same time becoming more porous. Indeed, these two developments go together. Their porousness means that they are more open to multinational migration; more of their members live the life of diaspora, whose center is elsewhere. In these circumstances, there is something awkward about replying simply, "This is how we do things here." This reply must be made in cases like the Rushdie controversy, where "how we do things" covers issues such as the right to life and to freedom of speech. The awkwardness arises from the fact that there are substantial numbers of people who are citizens and also belong to the culture that calls into question our philosophical boundaries. The challenge is to deal with their sense of marginalization without compromising our basic political principles. (63)

"We" are being swarmed by immigrants, illegals and refugees. "Our" cultures are constantly confronted with "theirs," are casting "our" settled cultural conversations into a disarray and flaunting differences. Moreover they want political rights to do so. Faced with this crisis, the last thing "we" need in Taylor's view is an entrenchment of "their" cultural demands enshrined in the constitution of the liberal state in the name of democracy. What "we" need to do instead is take the matter of "their" cultural demands to the level of civil society or community and plead for voluntary recognition on "our" part. "We" should do so because we do not want them to develop a crisis of self-identity which will exacerbate social disorder. But under no circumstances can "we" bring liberal procedural or legislative principles of equality into "our" cultural life and civil society. "We" should also refrain from making any statement of worth regarding "their" cultures.

Taylor's panic about the West's cultural crisis moving towards an impending civilizational doom is caused by his view of the non-western cultures' intrusions into "our" civil society or daily cultural life. This becomes most evident when we contrast this note of panic regarding third world cultures to the air of calm with which he speaks of Quebec's or francophone arguments about being a "distinct society." In *Reconciling the Solitudes* and "The Politics of Recognition" Taylor weighs the pros and cons of their cultural demands in a thoughtful and quiet manner. The reason for this calm is none other than the fact of their common European cultural origin and the prominent place held by the French language and culture in the European civilizational map, especially for elite intellectuals such as Taylor. But even there his anglo bias shows through, as he tells us that there is a lesson to be learned from the Meech Lake debacle, some conclusions to be drawn from it, which not only apply to the relation between Quebec and the rest of Canada, but also to the question of nationhood and culture of Canada as a whole (Taylor, 1994: 53-61). The moral which Taylor draws out from Meech Lake is that one cannot ride two horses at once. The francophones, or the Canadian non-anglo-Europeans, cannot evoke a principle of sameness, an abstract equality arrived at by shedding difference, in order to take part in the nation's polity, only to use that advantage of sameness to proclaim rights to cultural difference. But as the numbers of non-European diasporic others daily grow, and there are First Nations and long-dwelling Asians, Afro-Americans and Afro-Canadians as well, who are becoming progressively more politically assertive, the situation must be handled with care and subtlety, not force. In the event, there should be some recognition accorded to their ways of life involving their religions and other cultural practices. However, this must be done by avoiding the state apparatus, the route of legislation and so on, what Taylor calls a procedural form of liberal democracy.

The elite, authoritarian and patronizing import of Taylor's politics of recognition, especially in his advice to white or anglo-European Canadians, becomes particularly obvious if the shoes are switched, which means using the pronoun "we" for a diasporic "we," substituting the white "we" of Taylor's central subject. This other "they/we" has another cultural narrative. It is a historical tale of physical and cultural genocides, of colonial robbery of history and resources, of silences and marginalization. This narrative has as its context the very foundation of Canada, its methods of acquiring economic resources, of populating this colony, modes and regulations of labour importation and labour market, existence of these others in a racially ethnicized and legally constructed hierarchical form of citizenship. The cultural politics of this "they/we," that is their contestations on the ground of representation, expresses the totality of these relations and contexts. They are culturally and in every other way diminished by an ongoing subtle or overt racism which informs class or social formation in Canada. Taylor himself is aware of this "Canadian" resistance to cultural and social others — in himself and his ethnic compeers. As a result he reasons and reproves his "us" constituency, but only mildly, as a good christian father who is hosting foreign students at his family dinner would chide his misbehaving children. As long as the guest (worker) does not impose or force his/her culture on "us" with an air of assumed superiority, the gloves of consideration, recognition or tolerance, in short of good manners, can remain in place.

In teaching himself and his "us" constituency a degree of tolerance through the production of an argument for a voluntary recognition of the identity of the nation's or western civilization's others, Taylor has to carefully steer a line between not jeopardizing the centrality of anglo-European elite culture while offering some reasons for recognition which would persuade "us." As difference-blind liberalism with its argument of abstract equality is unacceptable to Taylor outside the sphere of the state, he must use another argument to convince "us." This argument, to be consistent with Taylor's attachment to a social order with difference, must find a non-liberal political ground to rehabilitate it. We cannot, obviously, return any more to the old world of difference, deference and preference or gainsay all of what has been achieved through modernity. So, how can one theorize a recognition which retains, or revives, an element of the old sense of cultural distinction and social order while also introducing a degree of voluntary acknowledgement which is uncompromised by a medieval code of

honour? Such a tolerance or recognition is not about an acceptance
of "their" cultures as a routine part of "ours," or about granting
"them" intrinsic cultural merits or rights. "They" are to be tolerated.
As Taylor puts it, at most "a case can be made for insisting on
universalization of *the presumption* that all cultures are of equal value
... if important consequences flow for people's identities from them"
(68).

Dubbing "their" cultures as "traditional" and responding
negatively to "their" politics of representation, which claims equal
value with "our" post-enlightenment ones, is reasonable. Taylor
says, "it can't make sense to demand as a matter of right that we
come up with a final concluding judgement that their multiculture's
value is great or equal to others"(69). And there are philosophical
or logical reasons on which "we" can refuse to make this judgement,
as difference and equality don't mix. "We" must not offer
multicultural others the hope that "we" can provide a neutral ground
on which people of all cultures can co-exist. Thus Taylor proceeds
to essentialize third world cultures as "traditional" and, as such,
religious, in contrast to both European post-enlightenment secular
as well as christian ones. He does not see these stances as equivalent
to making a cultural judgement, and instead refers to Gadamer's
idea of the necessity for a "fusion of cultural horizons" (67) in order
to make such a judgement. As "our" and "their" cultures have not
come to such a "fusion" yet, and thus, according to Taylor, occupy
exclusionary grounds, then "we" cannot simply make this gesture
dictated by a principle of ethics, claim value-neutrality, and thus
pretend to like them. Taylor then announces the redemptive ground
for "their" cultures: namely, that *all* cultures *may* have a marginal
value to contribute to identity formation, unless they are decadent
or of a partial milieu. This statement, surprisingly, does not strike
Taylor as being one of cultural judgement and also condescension.

Taylor's refusal to be a liberal in cultural matters and his belief
in the importance of culture for identity formation is elaborated in
this essay in the philosophical distinction between ethical and
aesthetic judgement. He refuses to conflate them, and contends
that to do so would be to make taste a politically actionable ground.
This transfer would be illegitimate and could not argue for cultural
rights ignoring the question of value, and thus engaging in a logical

contradiction with political consequences. It is interesting to note that Taylor's proscriptions and refusals apply only to the granting of cultural worth, but not to it's denial. He sees no judgement of worth or confusion of aesthetic and political judgement implicit in conferring elite European or anglo-North American cultures the status of Canadian national culture or world culture. A normalized colonial civilizational discourse holds sway over him. Moments in European history consisting of legislative silencing or augmenting of cultures from different regions, classes and sects are never really commented upon. But more importantly, Taylor refuses to see the class character of so-called European or Canadian culture itself. Any formative and ideological connection between the ruling or bourgeois classes and the dominant national culture, even when not enforced legislatively, escapes his notice. He fails to note not only that in the Canadian case the negative experiences of francophones could be seen as a matter of state discrimination, but also that this discrimination is indicative of the anglo elite cultural character of the ruling classes.

That the required philosophical distinction is constantly violated regarding alien cultures or cultures of underclasses, or that the formation of taste or aesthetic is integrally bound to history and politics, is obscure to Taylor because he is anti-marxist and even anti-Foucault and thus has no theory of ideology or hegemony. He therefore cannot see that the suspension of others' cultural worth is tantamount to asserting that of "ours" which is already in place, and that this expresses a power relation. This unseeing is the result of his acceptance of a theoretical separation between civil society (as cultural existence) and the state and public sphere, a separation which signals an adherence to social theorization. The cultural world, as Taylor sees it, is either devoid of social relations of power, or one where such relations, associated with cultural difference, have to be adjudicated at the level of civil society or the community. That such "communities" are differentially situated with regard to social power is not articulated within Taylor's theoretical horizon. As such he cannot find any partisanship in his contemptuous dismissal of both alien cultures and of white liberals who defend their worth as equal to European post-enlightenment cultures. He phrases their confusion in the following terms: "...[T]he act of declaring another culture's creation to be of worth and the act of declaring oneself on their side, even if their creations are not all that impressive, become indistinguishable" (69-70).

Charles Taylor's communitarian but elite multiculturalism may be liberal in social theorization, but it results in a scathing denunciation of liberalism's more crude and official variety. He accuses advocates of multicultural rights of lacking any sense of excellence or standard and criticizes their habit of converting cultural issues into those of "power and counter-power," thus creating between themselves and alien others "a nexus of hypocrisy" (70). These white liberal advocates are of the "us" group and, according to Taylor, harm the cause of others because they take "their" side, implicitly downgrading "our" culture. For Taylor they are not only hypocrites, pretending to consider something substandard as valuable, but also "frightfully condescending" and "disrespectful" (70). Taylor himself, however, holds a respectful and honest position towards others' cultures by a denial of their worth.

How then is there going to be a solution for cultural wars or dissatisfactions brewing at the level of civil society, which might plunge the western civilization into chaos? How is this tension and contestation on all sides to be managed or contained? If liberal judgements of equal worth are impossible, and the state may not interfere in matters of civil society, and the communities themselves are pitted adversarially, where should recognition come from? What can save "us" from the pitfalls of post-structuralist/post-modernist pseudo-solutions? This is where the philosophical moment, the moment of a transcendental and foundational principle, comes to help Taylor. We rise to the level of a universal hypothesis through *a presumption of worth*. On what ground must this presumption be made? Here he resorts to Herder, saying that religion could be the ground since it encodes an order of plenitude and great harmony, and as Taylor has already designated alien cultures as pre-modern or traditional and, as such, religious, we may *presume* some value in these religious cultures, since they have sustained these people for centuries. This means a dilemma of course for Taylor, as these religions are seen by him as essentially fundamentalist, and faces "us" with the possibility of situations arising such as that of Salman Rushdie. Does one condemn or condone a religion like islam? "One either forbids murder or allows it" (62). A terrible situation faces "us": what can "we" allow "them," how far can "we" let these fundamentalist religious cultures go? This dilemma notwithstanding, Taylor's own religious commitment prompts him to decide that even if "they" are horrible religious cultures and peoples, "we" must still continue to presume some sense of their worth — as long as this concession is not being forced out of "us" by some talk of rights, either by "them" or by some liberal "us," as long as it is "our" choice dictated by "our" philosophical tenets.

The reader is faced with the question, does this voluntary recognition hold as its foundational principle an element of self-recognition as well? It does indeed, because "we" recognize in "their" need of recognition "our" own need as well, to have "our" cultures respected for the purpose of "our" cultural identity formation. As "we" recognize "our" need in "their" mirror, "we" show ourselves as authentic identities as well as creatures capable of meeting moral obligations. With this philosophical gesture Taylor tries to close the gap between "we" and "they." A common "we" of a human kind emerges as "we," the humanity, are ideologically lifted into a philosopher's sphere outside of specificities, or maybe even of accidents, of history, actual social relations and politics. Believing this stance to be less abstract than the one held by liberals, Taylor offers cultural recognition in the place of multiculturalism.

Taylor sees his solution of voluntary recognition as a response to the identity needs of others, and this he considers to be their plea, a cry, requiring an apolitical solution. This apolitical perception is articulated by him from the very beginning as he disassociates culture from politics, which allows him to convert class struggle or rights struggles into pleas for recognition of one's cultural identity. If "they" themselves deny his interpretation Taylor for one is not taken in by what he considers to be spurious political talk. "They" are merely unable to know what "they" really want, thus the politics of social justice needs to be displaced by the politics of charitable recognition.

Though the issue of acknowledgment of identity should be closely connected to those of social subjectivity and political agency, Taylor does not consider his formulation or the solution for assuaging others' dissatisfaction to be a gesture of domination.

Unmindful of the power involved in arrogating upon himself the role of the interpreter who will tell us what is actually going on for others, Taylor deprives them of direct voices, political and social subjectivities. The bearers of these alien cultures are thus homogenized or essentialized into becoming unicultural and static ethnic identities. Secular or diverse cultural and religious beliefs and practices are impermissible for them. Political subjectivities and agencies ranging from liberalism, marxism, feminism to antiracism are inauthentic for them as they are, unlike the western "us," designated as essentially religious and pre-modern ethnic groups or cultures. Though Taylor pronounces that "we" cannot really know "their" cultures, no reader of "The Politics of Recognition" is left in doubt about how to think about "them." Thus arranging the world's cultures within a colonial discourse of tradition and modernity, and spatializing these characteristics with a "West and the rest" approach, Taylor makes as grand a cultural narrative and judgement as Hegel or Max Weber.[7]

What, then, happens to the malaise of modernity, a western theme which Taylor expatiates upon in *Hegel and Modern Society* or *Sources of the Self*? Particularly in the latter text we can see Taylor's ambivalence about modernity at its clearest when he is confronted with a choice between "western" and "eastern" cultures. Though he is often critical of the technological, utilitarian, individualistic rationality of modernity, when he compares European elite culture with what he considers to be "theirs," modernity unquestionably wins out. Taylor's immersion in the civilizational discourse, which we may also call a colonial discourse, makes him subscribe to the notion that cultures have essences. The cultural essence of the West is determined for him by christianity, which he sees as a source of modernity. Unlike islam with its imputed fundamentalist theocratic essence, christianity appears to him to be an open-minded, modernist belief system from its inception. Taylor's views on both christianity and islam, as well as on modernity, are worth quoting.

> For mainstream Islam, there is no question of separating politics and religion the way we have come to expect in Western liberal society. Liberalism is not a possible meeting ground for all cultures, but is the political expression of one range of cultures, and quite incompatible with other ranges. Moreover, as many Muslims are

well aware, Western liberalism is not so much an expression of
the secular, postreligious outlook that happens to be popular
among liberal *intellectuals* as a more organic outgrowth of
Christianity — at least as seen from the alternative vantage point
of Islam. The division of church and state goes back to the earliest
days of Christian civilization. The early forms of the separation
were very different from ours, but the basis was laid for modern
developments. The very term *secular* was originally part of the
Christian vocabulary. (62)

Taylor forgets, among other things, the Holy Roman Empire,
the Inquisition, the church's role in European colonization, and
instead claims the liberatory aspects of liberalism as christianity's
partial outgrowth. He feels that christianity is an ideal social form
and capable of self-questioning and self-correction, while islam,
for example, is irredeemably traditional-authoritarian. For Taylor
secular or rational thought is as though genetically programmed
into the cultural mind of the West, and is an impossible achievement
for the East. Curiously, Charles Taylor's projection of a
fundamentalist telos for islam is the same as that of the islamic
fundamentalist leaders themselves, who see themselves or their
version of islam as the true representatives of the faith and its
culture. The fate of Salman Rushdie, then, a sanctified proclamation
for his murder, seems lamentable but logical both from Taylor's
and Ayatollah Khomeini's standpoint. One wonders then about how
and why the *fatwwas* of the Vatican burning women and men as
heretics and witches through many centuries are not to be
considered the logical outcome of western christianity, or how to
even understand such practices and beliefs in the face of Taylor's
claim of an essential modernity for a western christianity.

We should perhaps look very briefly at the rights or liberal
theorists's disagreement with Charles Taylor. In his response to
Taylor's view on multiculturalism, Jürgen Habermas (Gutmann,
1994) has advocated that issues of identity and culture should not
especially become a matter of liberal democratic politics and its
state. The constitution and the legislative framework of the liberal
democratic state, which guarantee individual rights for freedom of
expression, speech and association, have enough provisions to deal

with denials and violations on an individual basis. Specific and traditional group cultures are not seen by Habermas to be of as great an importance as by Taylor, nor does he see it as the duty of the state to guarantee cultural survival. Habermas argues instead for a changeable nature of culture, and the possibility of everyone's absorption into a common liberal culture, brought about in the public space through debates and discussions and participation in the practices of citizenship. This is a secular, rational, political and public culture, not at the level of traditional life of the (religious) community, but one that emanates from the unfolding of liberal democracy and modernity. It is Habermas's view that non-Westerners can also become absorbed into this public culture.

Will Kymlicka, the most well-known liberal theorist of Canada, also speaks from within a liberal framework. He may be seen as the best example in terms of theorizing official multiculturalism in Canada, and links the discussion of cultural rights with group and individual rights. He tries to consider the nature and constitution of different cultural groups living in Canada within definitions of multi-nationality and poly-ethnicity. He offers proposals for cultural sovereignty of national (cultural) groups, such as the aboriginals and francophones, while emphasizing affirmative action and diversity orientations for poly-ethnic groups living in Canada, such as the South Asians, Chinese or Afro-Canadians. (Kymlicka, 1995)

Neither of these theorists give any serious thought to civil society, community, hegemony or ideology, while Taylor ignores the state as well as the hegemonic and ideological aspects of culture at the level of civil society or the community. Neither these unambiguous liberals nor the conservatively inflected liberal Taylor consider how social relations of power, spelling inequality, can form the ground for political organization of the national state. Thus issues of class, gender and "race," which are unimportant for Taylor, are also unimportant for "public culture" of Habermas, or for the liberal polity of Will Kymlicka, in spite of his references to difference as articulated by U.S. based black feminist legal theorists such as Iris Marion Young (1990). But for Kymlicka difference is a limited "cultural" rather than a political freedom. The deeper aspects of difference which encode racialized ethnicities within a patriarchal and class framework entirely escape him, as they do the others.

Ultimately then, both Taylor and the overt liberals rely on a radical public and private division of the organization of the social, and adopt an epistemological stance which disarticulates the practical-symbolic from the moral-aesthetic dimensions of life, and of both from the politico-economic.

It is this ideological, epistemic erasure of the integrity of the social that allows for a power-neutral culturalist rendition of difference. It obscures different kinds of differences, confusing cultural plurality with distinctions constructed upon relations and conceptual and cultural practices of power. We are thus prompted to forget that there are differences which come as cultural legacies of the non-Europeans, and which are negatively interpreted irrespective of their actual content when they enter into societies pre-textured with colonial and imperialist relations and ideologies. The variety of cultural-political practices that these alien(ated) others bring with them is in marked contrast to the uniformity that they are assigned or which begins to appear when they are subjected to a racist homogenization such as the one employed by Charles Taylor. It is this very process of subjection involving racist ascriptions which not only fuels demands for cultural rights, but also prompts fights at economic and general political levels. It is not a plea for recognition that "they" put forward, but rather a struggle to end exploitation and injustice. It is this politics which underlies even partial formulations of politics of representation.

I want to conclude by returning to the theme of Eurocentric self-referentiality that is implicit in Charles Taylor's politics of recognition, and point to the Hegelian dimension of his formulation. Here I would like to draw attention to Hegel's famous master-slave parable, and its applicability to how Taylor conceptualizes the notions of identity and recognition. Implicit in his advocacy for recognition is not just a plea for the identity of the slave, but rather his solution is more centrally directed at the *master's* identity. The type of recognition he suggests is a reflection of the master's self-centredness, his necessary interpellation of the slave in a dialectic of identity and recognition for his own need. If we now transpose this parable of identity from the master-slave relation to that between the "us" (European self and culture) and the "them" (non-European culture and self), the nature of Taylor's politics of recognition becomes clearer. If "they," or the multicultural communities, want recognition from "us," the hegemonic anglo-American elite culture, in order to be authentically identified as themselves, does not this serve a similar and a more urgent identity-creating process within ourselves? Could Europe and North America for the last few hundred years recognize themselves without their colonies, colonized and enslaved others, and their civilizational discourses? Is all this talk of recognition by Charles Taylor, in the end, a matter of "us," the hegemonic recognizer's self-validation, and done in the name of the identity need of others? By keeping the right to recognize or not at will, while denying the other the right to assert their identity through rights or other oppositional politics, do "we" use the politics of recognition as a device for entrenching the mastery of the master and the enslavement of the slave? Does the moment of others' plea for recognition, then, amount to the creation of a mirror for self-gazing?

This question brings us to making a link between Charles Taylor's politics of recognition and Hegel's theory of history, in which the Spirit-self or the Idea seeks its own fullness of identity through the medium of its alienation into the other. As a philosophical proposition or a mode of speculative thought there is nothing either particularly uplifting or objectionable about this statement. But when translated into socio-historical relations, into political philosophy, this metaphysical parable can become a disturbing possibility and practice. It is disturbing because these others, the aliens with their alien cultures, who are perceived as alienated emanations of the elite European/North American selves, are actual people, not ideas. They have substantive and complex histories, societies and cultures. They are as complex and contradictory cultural entities and identities as "us," the supposed recognition givers. Unboxed from the paradigm of tradition and modernity, the aliens of the West are people with histories, with social relations and ideologies of power among themselves. Class, gender, caste, "race" and religion make them far from homogeneous, and similar to those among whom they find themselves. They are as secular and rational or as religious or traditional as Taylor's "we." The identity of their politics need not only be the politics of identity.

We expect more from a state and society designated as modern or liberal democratic than christian moral and cultural platitudes about "our" obligation of recognition. Nor do we expect cultural reductions and judgements regarding the content of cultures in the name of logical argument. What is necessary to deal with cultural contestation, therefore, is not an accolade of worth, or a statement of their equal value, but rather a political organization, even constitutional reforms, which guarantee structural and legal conditions to all members of the society to wage struggles at many levels, including that of culture. These struggles are meant to free people as a whole from the necessity of seeking recognition from a hegemonic self, and from the possibility of their having the power to grant it. Charles Taylor may find this proposal unbelievable, an example of a false consciousness which speaks about injustice when all it wants is to go back to a modern day form of an older society of difference — a recognition from the patron. But whatever Taylor's thoughts on this topic may be, many — women, non-white or third world peoples, gays and lesbians or underclasses — will not want from him or "us" this recognition which he so kindly offers. This refusal by "them" is not a refusal of mutuality or universal respect. It is a refusal of an elitist form of self-deception, which in the name of the community offers condescension. Recognition needs respect and dignity, its basic principle is accepting the autonomy of the other, and being honest about power relations which hinder this autonomy.

NOTES

1 See for example Taylor (1993: 46-48, 136) and Taylor (1994: 30-32).

2 See Taylor (1989: 10), where he characterizes his text as "an essay of retrieval."

3 See also Taylor (1994: 52-54) on the theme of Americanization of liberal politics in this context.

4 For Taylor on the movement between pre-modern and post-modern times see (1994: 44-51); on abstract individualism, see (1994: 36). In this context, see also Taylor on the theme of Americanization of liberal politics (1994: 52-54).

5 Taylor 1994: 37-38. There is a move seen here from politics of equal recognition and dignity to that of a liberal politics of difference.

6 In *Sources of the Self* (1989: 202-204) Taylor tells us what he thinks of marxism. Seemingly speaking to "over-simple and reductive variants" or "vulgar marxism," this chapter entitled "Digression of Historical Explanation" tells us of no other kind, in fact leaving us with the view that to be a marxist is to be reductive and vulgar.

7 For Hegel and Weber on India see Ronald Inden (1990) and Ramila Thapar (1993).

REFERENCES

Gramsci, Antonio. *Selections from the Prison Notebooks.* Trans. and ed. Quentin Hoare and Geoffrey Nowell Smith. New York: International Publishers, 1971.

Gutmann, Amy. *Multiculturalism: Examining the Politics of Recognition.* Princeton, New Jersey: Princeton University Press, 1994.

Inden, Ronald. *Imagining India.* Oxford: Blackwell, 1990.

Kymlicka, Will. *Multicultural Citizenship: A Liberal Theory of Minority Rights.* Oxford: Clarendon Press, 1995.

Macpherson, C. B. *The Life and Times of Liberal Democracy.* Oxford: Oxford University Press, 1977.

Marx, Karl and Frederick Engels. *The German Ideology.* Ed. C. J. Arthur. New York: International Publishers, 1973.

Smith, Dorothy E. *The Everyday World as Problematic: A Feminist Sociology.* Toronto: University of Toronto Press, 1987.

Taylor, Charles. *Hegel and Modern Society.* Cambridge: Cambridge University Press. 1979.

———. *Sources of the Self: The Making of Modern Identity.* Cambridge, Massachusetts: Harvard University Press, 1989.

———. *Reconciling the Solitudes: Essays on Canadian Federalism and Nationalism.* Montreal and Kingston: McGill-Queen's University Press, 1993.

———. "The Politics of Recognition." In *Multiculturalism: Examining the Politics of Recognition,* ed. Amy Gutmann, 25-74. Princeton, New Jersey: Princeton University Press, 1994.

Thapar, Ramila. *Interpreting Early India.* Delhi: Oxford University Press, 1993.

Young, Iris Marion. *Justice and the Politics of Difference.* Princeton, New Jersey. Princeton University Press, 1990.

CHAPTER 5

A Question of Silence:
Reflections on Violence Against
Women in Communities of Colour

Calcutta, 15 November 1997

Dear Ena and Angela,
Breaking with scholarly protocols, I am writing this piece as a letter to you
because what I want to say needs an embodied reader. The topic is too close
to our everyday life and politics to come wrapped in a package of academic
or theoretical abstractions. Thank you for asking me to write, and for
accepting a piece that is more reflection than definitive research. Thank
you also for being my ideal readers through whom I can speak to others.

I

*I*ssues of patriarchy and violence against women are disturbing in general, but they become even more so when considered in relation to our so-called own communities. I am speaking of South Asian communities about which I know most, but what I have to say may apply to "other" Canadian communities which are non-white.[1] I know that violence against women is a pervasively present phenomenon among us, in spite of much talk about honour and respect for women, including deification of the feminine principle as claimed by the hindus. I also know that not only I, but large numbers of women, have been in a position to know of instances of violence of various degrees, and have not known what to do or where to speak about it. We have often spoken among ourselves in a private or personal capacity, and sometimes we have expressed our concerns publicly. I have been haunted by the story of a Sri Lankan woman who killed her two daughters and attempted suicide. These events are not, as far as I can understand, a matter of personal pathology — they have to be informed with a consideration of her migration, her isolation, her lack of economic and social support, an extremely abusive marriage, and a sexist and racist host society, where hospitals continue to neglect signs of violence against women. On a lesser scale, we worry about women who leave the temporary refuge of the shelters for their "homes," returning to the same partners whose violence drove them out in the first place. But in spite of our general concern and common knowledge, I have not read anything extensive or substantial on the phenomenon of violence against women within their so-called communities — communities which are constituted by outside forces with (rather than by) "people of colour." Perhaps there is writing coming out of the United Kingdom or United States, but it has not gained enough prominence to attract public attention.

So, as things stand now, a direct critical assessment, social analysis, or political project on this issue has not been undertaken. We seem to have left this task mainly to poets and fiction writers, whose business we think it is to deal with experience. And as you know, as social scientists we have been taught to regard experience with extreme suspicion as a source for reliable social knowledge. Even though certain types of feminist theorists have sought to valorize experience, the current discursivism of feminist theories has put a big question mark against experience, against actual lives as they are lived by women. But rendered into literary or cultural artifacts and relegated to the borderlands of fact and fiction, what we know and say about community violence against women does not create the same pressure for address or redress as it would if we had to admit that this violence is a direct part of our diasporic reality. We would then have to speak to and act on patriarchal violence within our homes, within the moral or social regulation of the very modalities of constituting "the community." As things are, we maintain a public silence, even if we know it only rebounds on us negatively. We need to explore this silence, to ask what our investment in it might be. This is precisely what I am trying to do in this letter, as well as to speak to the nature of patriarchal violence within the terrain of our domestic lives.

We cannot even begin to plumb the depth of this silence unless we recognize its complex character. As you know, silence is highly telling — it can mean anything from complicity to resistance. Its presence, in the shape of an absence in public discourse about violence against women in South Asian or other non-white communities, speaks volumes about our political and socio-cultural organization and stance. And even though this silence creates large holes in the fabric of our public political culture, that which we have not addressed directly seeps out, is displaced or slips into other concerns or issues. The repressed returns, as it were, in court cases, in refugee and immigration hearings, in women's shelters, changing individual and private instances into examples of public and collective lives.

One of the reasons for this paradoxical silence may be that public utterance puts us in a situation of responsibility — it makes us accountable to and for others and ourselves. After all, what we say in print, in any public medium, is fixed in form, content, and time. It becomes part of an acknowledged, even official reality, liable to be seen as a distinct political position. We are no longer just overheard or peeped into. The doors of the community open as we speak "out." So, obviously, we are wary, not only about what we say in public, but where and how we say it. We want to assess the location and reception of our public statements, our disclosures and discussions in the arena of social communication. We are, if anything, overly sensitive towards the ideological strands or networks into which they will be woven, how our statements will be received by those who are not "us," particularly those "others" who consider us not as people, but as "ethnic communities." These are not unimportant considerations for those who hold not only "minority," but "visible minority," status in a white and christian majoritarian nation state. But then we are in a situation of double jeopardy, since speaking and not speaking both entail problems. In fact, we may be better off breaking this silence, since this articulation itself is a political act giving rise to other political possibilities. But going public in this matter requires that we are able to expose and critique the patriarchal constitution of our communities, which is the same as all other communities, without too much squeamishness about our dirty laundry.

II

To put forward our critique regarding violence against women in our communities, we cannot begin by taking the concept of "community" for granted. We need to remember that it is a political and cultural-ideological formation reliant upon social relations which are the base of social life, and not a spontaneous or natural association of people. This constructed and contingent nature of the concept of community is important to keep in mind, since it is becoming increasingly common in social sciences to treat this concept, along with a definite article or an adjective, as a natural, almost an instinctive, form of social and cultural association. Cultural anthropology, with its various types of relativism, seems to have been an important source for this practice of considering "community" as a self-contained and natural formation, a social given, which may be interchangeable with the concept of civil society.

But if, instead of naturalizing "community," we see it as a formation, an ideological, that is, cultural and political practice, it becomes possible for us to develop a critique of the social organization, social relations, and moral regulations which go into the making of it. We can then begin to see that a group of people with a language, a religion, or an interest in common may only become an identifiable and stable social and political structure — in spite of the presence of power relations among them — through a combination of internal and external factors. It is in their interaction of contradiction and convergence that a so-called community is formed. This community, as in the case of women and on issues of gender and patriarchy, can only hold itself together by maintaining a silence about issues of power. A community is also formed both on grounds of difference and commonness. The difference is

obviously from those who lack features in common, and therefore
are "others" to the collective "self" of the community, usually a
smaller group marked out as different by the majority. This makes
the community into a minoritarian concept, one whose political and
social roots lie in being collectively marked out as different from
the hegemonic group. It is not difficult to understand this process
of community formation when we see the different ways in which
the Canadian state and hegemonic common sense mark out their
social "others." This othering implies racism, ethnicization (with a
"race" component), and homogenization. People who are thus
"othered" also bond together *vis à vis* these designatory processes
in a defensive move, while being penned within a political and
cultural boundary. Silence regarding malpractices within these
stereotypically constructed and defensively self-constituted
communities is therefore not unexpected.

Inscribed and instituted politically from the outside, the
communities themselves also suppress internal sources of division
and seek to present themselves, at least in their representational
endeavours, as seamless realities. Silence, therefore, regarding class,
gender, and other power relations, characterizes this voluntary
aspect of community making as well. And as we shall see later, the
technology for constructing differences relies on the concept of
tradition, which is implicated in both aspects of community
formation. This is what characterizes these communities as
traditional, in contradistinction to the "modernity" of the
"Canadians," the second half of this binary paradigm. This
construction of traditionality is then fleshed out with the invention
of particular traditions — relevant for different nationalities and
cultural groups. Needless to say the notion of a traditional
community rests explicitly on patriarchy and on severely gendered
social organization and ideology. These are legitimated as an essence
of the identity of these communities. This traditional (patriarchal)
identity, then, is equally the result of an othering from powerful
outside forces and an internalized Orientalism and a gendered class
organization.

Keeping these processes of community formation in view —
disputing its natural and synonymous status as and with civil society
— we can begin our critique by invoking our general membership

as women of these communities. We need to remember that we are the "others" of white women in the Canadian national imaginary, and this is connected with the fact that we are an integral part of the peoples who were brought as indentured workers, or migrated to Canada from former colonies under severe economic conditions created by post-colonial imperialism. Unlike European or white women, we present "Canada" with the problem of inassimilation. We are simultaneously essentialized into homogenized yet racialized and ethnicized subjects, whose actual differences are drowned in the multicultural discourse of diversity. We are worried, understandably, to speak of "our" brutalities and shortcomings, because of not being even minimally in control of the public and political domains of speech or ideological construction. The pre-existence of a colonial/racist/Orientalist perception and stereotypes of us, embedded in official and everyday structural and cultural practices and meanings, have been powerful sources of distortion and misrepresentation of our subjectivities and politics. This, of course, is not only true of Canada but of elsewhere in the West as well. This sexist-racist common sense, with its pervasive presence in the political economy and dominant culture of Canada, is rooted in a history of colonial conquests, genocides and ongoing projects of profit and rule. This is productive of an ethos of European or white supremacy which provides the political conscious or unconscious of Canada's nation state and political-cultural space. We are simultaneously present and absent in these spaces, and in the apparatus of the state. It is this paradox of presence and absence, of difference and sameness (as some sort of members of this Canadian nation), that multiculturalism both constructs and augments. Our political and social identities are contingent upon this. We might say that the reasons both for our presence in Canada and for the official discourse of multiculturalism are connected to our actual absence in and abdication of public space and speech regarding ourselves and our communities' horrendous treatment of women.

The situation is complicated. But how can it be any different, when we come from colonial and imperialist histories and presents and find ourselves in the midst of a white settler colony struggling to transform itself into a liberal democracy? Canada's participation in imperialism on the coat tails of the United States is not hidden from public view. Inhabiting this terrain, our refugee and immigrant statuses mark us as second-class citizens, if citizens at all. We stand, both men and women, uncertainly at the edge of "Canada," the nation. Comprehended in this political economy, a racialized class organization which is as much about whiteness as blackness, we step back in time. We are recolonized, directly — and that isn't just speaking metaphorically. Coming from countries which have seen anti-colonial struggles in one form or another and shaken off direct colonial rule, we put ourselves back into socio-political spaces closely resembling a colony — at least where we are concerned. Here we are marked by a difference which has less to say about us — our histories and cultures — than about a mode of socio-political interpretation within a pre-established symbolic and practical schema of a racialized or ethnicized colonial and slave-owning discourse.

It is at the receiving end of this proliferation of denigrating differences and homogenization that the incoming "others" go through their community formation. Of course, at the same time they are going through a process of class formation as well, which is creating a difference among themselves, as much as between them and "Canadians." But the discourse of community cannot and is not meant to express or accommodate that. In the ideological discourse of "the community" it was made to appear that when people migrated, they did so as communities, not as responses to national and international political economy.

We can say, therefore, that there is nothing natural about communities. In fact they are contested grounds of socio-cultural definitions and political agencies. Contradictory processes of creating "us" and "them" are at work in them, and we have here a situation of mini-hegemonies confronting and conforming to a national ideological hegemony. Form and content of communities reflect this, and we continue to be constructed and excluded by the same overarching hegemony. This becomes evident when we look at the discourse and workings of official multiculturalism, in which where we are from, as nationalities and cultures — Jamaica, Vietnam, or India — matters very little when we are being distinguished from "Canadians," while our specific differences provide the stepping stones for this general difference. We know very quickly that we are not "them" or "Canadians," while our "us" can cross national boundaries, and sometimes it does. Racism, Eurocentrism, or ethnocentrism, which impacts on all non-whites in this way, generates a space for a broader community among us, creating a ground for anti-racism. But this again is not a given or a foregone conclusion, since internalized racism or community boundaries generally help create a closed in socio-cultural space and a highly fragmented political agency. So while there is in this mechanism of mass exclusion, called multicultural community, room for the excluded to unite irrespective of their different regional and individual histories, languages, and religions, the unity in actuality has not been more than that of region, religion, and perhaps language. In fact, regional and linguistic communities seem to be in the process of fast alternation on the ground of religion — thus being "hindus" and "muslims" has currently become alarmingly relevant. This deepening of traditionality has not boded well for women among these communities.

So, possibilities for a community of the excluded notwithstanding, we have been docile with regard to the political economy of Canada. We have by and large uncritically inhabited the socio-economic zones, grids, or boxes created for us by Manpower and Immigration or Employment and Immigration Canada. We have been legally bonded and bounded. This boundary, invisible though inexorable, is the outer wall of the community — whatever that may be — and it not only keeps others "out," but us "in." From this point of view community is not only an ideological and social category, but also a category of the state. This becomes evident if we reflect on the role of this category in the mode of administering the civil society, for example, in electoral politics, in organizing the labour market, in social assistance or cultural funding.

You might at this point object to this non-cultural way of reading the socio-genetics of the concept of community, which goes against the grain of conventional use of the term. You might refer to the role that our own ethnocultural varieties and differences play in the making of communities. You might want to speak of religions, languages, social customs — the semiotic and moral constructions and regulations that we identify ourselves by. Are we not marked as communities in these terms, making "us" distinct from others? These would be, or should be, our questions if we were to read the "community" as an equivalent for the civil society. But as I have pointed out, communities are formed through the pressure of external forces far more than for reasons of cultural expression. There is no reason for the inhabitants of any region to engage in an exercise of collective self-identification unless there is the presence of a dominant group which is ascribing certain definitions and identity markers onto them. This process of complex and contradictory interactions between external and internal forces, which I have already spoken to, makes it evident that "community" is a very specific way of politicizing and organizing cultural particularities of social groups. In this it is no different from the use of the concept of caste or religion with which the colonial powers created administrative and ruling regimes in the colonies.

Questioning the status of the community as a natural, social formation does not automatically imply a dismissal of points of commonality among peoples of different regions, cultural habits, nationalities, and histories, or, for that matter, among religious groups from those regions. It is true that such people often tend to seek each other out, to speak the same language, eat the same food, or display fashions. Very often in the earlier part of their existence in Canada it is a survival necessity for learning the ropes in the new country, getting employment or business contacts, and so on. But if the Canadian society into which they come were non-threatening and non-exclusive, if racism were not a daily reality, this stage of cultural bonding would be short, and more fluid than it is at present. In that case cultural practices would not harden into "identities" or ethnic typologies, but temporary stages of social becoming, both at individual and collective levels. Such elective affinities or cultural associations cannot be called communities, which imply organization and institutionalization — a mechanism for a rigid cultural reproduction. Voluntary cultural associations are both temporary and much less organized, and often a very small part of the existence of people. This is evident if we observe the European or white immigrants who may live in ethnic networks, for example the Italians or Ukrainians, but who did not ossify into permanent communities with fixed and branded identities.

Things are different with us, that is, non-white immigrants —
even if we are conversant in English or French, which people from
South Asia, Africa, and the Caribbean generally are. With them the
process is reversed, since they come as individual migrants and
slowly harden into the institutional form of the community. The
reason for this, I am afraid, is not what is inside of them, but rather
in their skin. Their skin is written upon with colonial discourse —
which is orientalist and racist. Thus memories, experiences, customs,
languages, and religions of such peoples become interpreted into
reificatory and often negative cultural types or identities. The
political process of minoritization accompanies this interpretive
exercise, and together they lead to the formation of communities.
When we speak of "diversity" it is this set of reified and politicized
differences that we are invoking, and they provide the basis for
ethnocultural identity and politics of representation.

That communities are not simple self-projections of cultural
groups, but rather, inherently political formations, is something
we need to keep in mind. This is particularly important in the last
two decades, when a discourse of community and cultural diversity
has been engraved into the Canadian body politic. This is not just
at the level of society at large, but in the official formulation and
implementation of multiculturalism. Though it may strike one as
curious that any "ism" can be made out of culture (we don't, after
all, talk of "culturalism" as state policy), we do live in an era when
political and ideological stances are created and institutionalized
out of features of everyday life or cultures (especially of non-white
people). Entire administrative apparatuses are alerted to cultural
characteristics of non-white/non-Europe "others," extending from
law and policing to mental health and labour. Such cultural "isms"
and their practicalization in the context of ruling and administration
cannot but need and create essentialist characteristics in the interests
of stability and predictability. If the groups were not to be seen as
homogeneous in terms of possessing these essential traits, no
administration could be put in place. Difference and diversity would
not then be effective categories for deployment in ruling, but indeed
contrary to it.

We might ask at this point a question or two regarding the
content of these putative differences and diversities. Is this content

entirely invented? Are they simply baseless, imagined essentialities? The answer to this question points us towards the epistemology implied in the creation of all ideological categories, as elaborated by Marx, and best discussed in *The German Ideology*. It is not that ideology invents particular socio-cultural features, found among many, but rather it centres some and erases others which might contradict the centrality of the selected ones. These selected features do not exist as discrete or floating pieces, but rather assume a categorical status by an extraneous connection which is established among them, often in a causal or positive mode. In other words, a discursive mode is established which creates falsehood, we might say, by a particular arrangement of existing characteristics. It is the whole discursive organization that is distortive or untrue, not particular features as such, and it is in their establishment as "essential" that the harm is most palpable. This ideological activity of consciousness has been called power/knowledge when particularly annexed to the project of ruling. Critique of colonial discourse, now so frequently practised, provides us with more than ample examples of this. It is there we see that paradigms, such as that of civilization and savagery or tradition and modernity, offer the discursive terrain or interpretive schema for understanding or representing cultural traits of colonized or enslaved peoples. It is from this source that the content of difference and diversity of official multiculturalism evolves. This reduces non-Europeans the world over into pre-modern, traditional, or even downright savage peoples, while equating Europeans with modernity, progress, and civilization. The social ethos and cultural identities of the "others" of Europe are presumed to be religious, their conduct ritualistic, and their temperament emotional and unruly. They are at once civilizationally ancient (and therefore in decay) and primitive (therefore undeveloped). These are the ideological underpinnings of the not so benign discourse of multicultural diversity. This is difference and representation as constructed through historical and social relations of power, and it leads to the making of a selective constellation of cultural attributes and ideological packages which contour and control the multicultural community.

This, then, is the ascriptive or normative process through which multicultural communities come to life and into political play in relation to state repression and conditional or limited rewards. Furthermore, we have a situation here of double reification, which combines communitization from above (state and dominant ideology or hegemonic common sense) and from below (from the subject populations themselves). These reified collectivities of difference create a situation of unofficial apartheid, a general culture of apartheid in the overall socio-cultural terrain of the country. Essentialized cultural identities already in place are rigidly maintained, while the general culture of apartheid proliferates fragmented and enclosed cultural territories which are both officially and voluntarily maintained. Political participation of non-white immigrants or their political subjectivities or agencies are increasingly conceived and conducted on these bases. The concept of community and its organization, then, provide the articulating bases between people and the state.[2]

III

These complexities of community formation provide us the problematic within which patriarchal violence, in its various manifestations, has to be grounded. We must remind ourselves here of the pervasive presence of patriarchy and specific forms of gender organization in all societies of our present day world, and of their long historical presence. Both general social organization and specific forms of ruling, of creating hegemonies, require this gendering and patriarchy as ideological and moral regulation. Whether this patriarchy is intrinsic and biologically based or contingent need not detain us here. What is important is that they have been historically in place for a very long time. The incoming peoples about whom we have been speaking come from spaces as deeply patriarchal and gender organized as the social space they enter into in Canada. They do not learn patriarchal violence after coming here. They also come from a social organization and politics of class, from national hegemonic systems, all of which are organized by gender and patriarchy. Class and gender, seemingly two distinct systems of oppression, are only so in theory — in practice they constitute and mediate each other in a network of overall social relations of power. White or not, immigrants and "Canadians" all live in this gendered and classed social reality. So violence against women, latent or blatant, is not surprising among communities which have, like all other social groups, all the social conditions for this and other patriarchal forms of violence, such as homophobia. Misogyny, an extreme form of patriarchy, cannot be discussed here in detail — but it should suffice to point out that the homosexual male has long been feminized, and the lesbian seen as a masculinist, female aberration. The hatred for both contains, on the one hand a displaced hatred for women, and on the other an anger or even hatred for those who invert the patriarchal social norm of heterosexuality. Unlike the artificial divide instituted between the West and the rest, there is in fact a deep commonality between them in matters pertaining to these hegemonic norms, and regarding practices and ideologies of property and class. What, then, is the specificity of violence against women within the confines of the community?

The answer to this question refers us back to the point I made about recolonization, which occurs when people of former colonies return to direct white rule by coming to the West. Class and gender organization and normative behaviour undergo a peculiar twist in this situation. On the one hand the process of internalization of colonial values, such as of racism, is intensified and projected through self hatred and anti-Black racism; on the other hand, this submission gesture is refuted or compensated by gestures of resistance. They revive and develop further a certain kind of nationalism, with some features in common with the nationalism of formerly colonized countries. This can happen very easily as these non-white, non-European communities function like mini-cultural nationalities in this recolonizing context. They seize upon the mainstream's and the state's tendencies and rules to differentiate them, and adopt these cultural differences. They proclaim these differences to be substantive and inherent, and proclaim their cultural autonomy in the face of an ethics of assimilationism while seeking to become political agents within the same framework of ideologies and institutions. Their resistance, what there is of it, is mostly cultural, and typically minority politics, which cannot and does not aspire to state formation, unlike anti-colonial nationalisms.

In this surrender-submission dialectic they rely mainly on colonial discourse, especially as they are from "the East." The main idea that they carry over with themselves and deepen on the Western soil is their self-characterization as "traditional." From this stance they engage in self-reification as a collective group, and develop logically their self-projection as religious, anti- and pre-modern peoples. They evoke mythical pasts or histories to support their current ideological stances, and create a politics internal to their definition of community which relies extensively on patriarchal moral regulations. This invention of tradition legitimizes and institutionalizes them as clients of the state, while the essentialist logic of community formation homogenizes all into one, and a few can represent the rest to the state and the world at large.

The community, as we can see, is a very modern formation, as is cultural nationalism. Its appeal to tradition, i.e. religion and antiquity, are its passwords into some limited space in the realms of power. To speak authoritatively in a representational capacity it is therefore imperative to speak in moral terms. This is most effectively done through a religious discourse and related practices of moral regulation. It requires in particular an absolute subscription to feudal or semi-feudal patriarchies, as well as the erasure of class, as this leads to social conflicts. All this provides a situation of surplus repression for women, sexual "others," as well as for people of lower class standing — all in the way of creating communities. Hierarchy and patriarchy as natural or divinely ordained conduct allows for a peculiar situation where class and gender power are both vindicated and occluded at once. Domination of women, of sexual "others," and subordination of children take on here the character of duties that each male head of the family and the male leaders of the community, who may also be religious heads, must perform. Patriarchal social violence is thus daily and spiritually normalized in these walled towns of communities or religious and cultural ghettoes.

What is put forward by the communities as assertion of difference, as resistance, often turns out to be colonial discourse with reversed valuations. In this context, tradition is considered in a highly positive light, while modernity, rationalism, and social criticism are negatively valorized. Religious fundamentalism is considered a particularly authentic sign of our Easternness. This is mini-cultural nationalism writ small, within a larger national imaginary, putting up its barricades and political signs with a neo-colonial inflection. This situation is not new. In the context of development of one strand of nationalism in India, among the hindu petty bourgeoisie, we have already seen this situation on a much larger scale. Many scholars and critics, feminists and others, have remarked on the peculiar importance of the sign of woman, as mother in particular, and of the feminization of the land or country as mother-goddess. These ideological manoeuvres have little to do with women, except to indicate their property or service role to the nation. The same could be said of the use of women and familial regulations pertaining to the ideological positioning of the community.

IV

The vested interests of upwardly mobile males, with religious patriarchal power in their hands, either in these types of communities or in nationalist projects, makes it difficult to question the imputed homogeneity or unity of the community. "Divisive" issues of gender and class, or for that matter of internalized colonial discourse or racism, cannot therefore be broached without enormous resistance and silencing from within. In formulating the interest of women and the causes of their oppression, no matter how aware of and informed with other social relations of power, we thus need to step back from the ideological and political schema of the community. Furthermore, we need to speak about patriarchy in inter- and intra-class terms, even at the risk of being misunderstood as separatist feminists, because it involves being "disloyal" to our so-called civilizations or national cultures.

If we do take this "disloyal" stance, which is the only real critical stance we can take, we can see that a cognizance of patriarchy and gender is also a cognizance of class and property relations in general. It is this that patriarchal or male perception cannot see or tolerate. Their resistance to colonial or national domination has never been questioning of either property or patriarchy. This is where their male and petty bourgeois or bourgeois class character is fully visible. This does not mean that mini-cultural nationalities or political collectives do not engage in class politics, but they do so, fully though implicitly, with the purpose of upward mobility rather than in the interest of social and economic equality. They are part of the phenomenon of class formation, and display the same characteristics as did the bourgeoisie in their earliest years of state formation, when they spoke in the name of all. It is then that they created theories of democracy and liberalism, which they were unable to actualize due to their class interests. In this commitment to an ethics of possession and politics of property, where property includes labour power and physical or reproductive capacities, the "others" of metropolitan capitalist democracies are in no way different from the mainstream, though their operational modalities may be highly situation specific.

In this erasure of class and gender, in protecting property and its proprieties, the "traditional" communities and the "modern" Canadian state show a remarkable similarity and practical convergence. Through the state's need to create an apparatus of political interpellation of "others," official multiculturalism came into being. This could then create political agencies through the various modalities of development of multiculturalism, whose ideology is refracted in the language and practices of diversity and implementation of institutional projects. Neither class nor gender, which are differences created through social relations of power, nor "race," another of these excruciating constructs of power, could be raised as issues within this discourse of diversity and redressed. In fact, what counted as difference were so-called cultural differences, and the project was aimed at preaching "tolerance" to the majority while leaving relations of power unchallenged either among them or among the objects of their tolerance. An intensification of class, gender, and patriarchy was encouraged through multicultural identifications, since the "others" were deemed "traditional" (i.e. patriarchal, hierarchical, and religious) and thus "natural" practitioners of these inequalities. Criticisms of abuse of women in the community, even when brought into the court, fell prey to "cultural" or "religious" legal arguments.

This continues to be the case. Definitional boundaries which are vital for legal and social jurisdiction of the Canadian state, which is as thoroughly "traditional" in these matters as the immigrants, rest on these essentialization gestures. It suits the Canadian state just as much as it suits the elite in the communities to leave intact these traditions and rituals of power. That the community is a political-ideological construct, particular to history and a politics, and therefore ignores the real diversities among people migrating from "other" countries, can have no place in this scheme of things. Progressive and critical people among these immigrants are thus dubbed atypical, Westernized, and inauthentic to their culture, both by the leading conservative elements among them and by their progenitor protector, the Canadian state. Violence against women or sexual "others," aggressive and hateful attitudes towards the religion of others, especially towards islam, become the bedrock of normal community identity. Oppression of women and feudal (rather than bourgeois) patriarchy thus become "our" social being, and such behaviour earns or maintains a colonial or racist contempt for us, while being treated permissively by the state. This deprives women of legal and political recourse and social assistance. On the other hand, the same type of characterization also deprives muslim males in Canada, particularly from Arab countries, of legal justice, since the community as a whole is tarred with the brush of fanaticism.

Communities, or the elite of these mini-nationalities, of course play their card of cultural difference according to dictates. They too, in spite of their anti-liberal stance, separate culture from all other social moments, such as that of economy. Equating "culture" with religion, and making a particularly elite brand of that religion the fountainhead of all ethical and customary values, they too assert the master script and make no fundamental socio-economic demands. Through the mask of pre-modernity and anti-materialism they participate most effectively in a capitalist state of a highly modern nature. In return for proclaiming a primordial traditionality they are left alone as rulers of their own communities, to rule over women, sexual "others," the economically dispossessed, and children. The social space of countries they migrate from or flee as refugees becomes a state of mind rather than a place in history.

The political and cultural conflicts raging in South Asia, Egypt, Algeria or Latin America, for example, where secularism and religious fundamentalism are in struggle, are altogether erased. A totalizing myth of tradition engrosses entire land masses, in fact two-thirds of the world, which foundationally rests on patriarchy. This is the imputed and self-proclaimed organic unity or wholeness of communities!

When we look at the status of women in the communities, we find it to be one of "property," of belonging to individual male heads of families as well as to the institutions called the family and the community. The morality of a collective organic nature seems to apply to them, whereas males are encouraged to individualism and entrepreneurialism in their very definition of masculinity. This control over women as a community's property, the object of patriarchal command, is not only traditional or god-given, but this sacred authority is actualized and reinforced by the secular construction and sanction of the Canadian state. The legal category of "the head of the family," with all the prerogatives and responsibilities pertaining to it, is entirely a category of state-delegated power to men. It is a category that extends from "immigrants" to "Canadians," and offers men who hold this position practically a life-and-death power over women and children. This has been discussed specially with regard to "sponsored immigrants," generally wives, who are held at the mercy of their husbands since they have no legal rights in Canada independent of their relationship with their husbands. The threat of deportation that hangs over their head — the loss of livelihood, displacement, separation from children, and social disgrace that might result from a breakdown of sponsorship — is a violent and volatile one. This is what makes innumerable women stay with their husbands in dangerous and humiliating situations, or to return to their so-called homes. Any challenge to the cultural identity of being "traditional," which means questioning religious and patriarchal injunctions, cannot be very effectively mounted from such a vulnerable socio-economic location. If this law were to have been amended, and wives of immigrating husbands could be seen as independent political and legal adults, not as their dependents, we might have seen something quite different from "traditional" behaviour. It is then that we would have known whether muslim women veil themselves because they want to, or because they are made to under conditions of subtle and overt duress. As it is we have no way of knowing their real will, since they are subject to what is called "multiple" but also converging patriarchies of the community male elite and the Canadian state. Facile anti-racism or cultural nationalism simply offers a window-dressing of legitimation.

To return to a theme introduced earlier, we might say that women's status as a "sign" or even a symbol for "our" cultural autonomy amounts to no more than being handmaidens of god, priest, and husband. This subordination or domination is mediated and regulated through the patriarchal family code, and anchored to the moral regulations of honour and shame. Any deviance from the domestic patriarchy of family (extended into wider kinship networks), from strict heterosexist codes, is a pathway to shame and punishment. This may range from censure to physical violence and social ostracism by the community. Women, and involved men, who help to bring about sexual disgrace may even be killed. The cases of killings of "deviant" women in Vancouver — for example, a woman who left her community by developing an emotional and sexual attachment outside of it — may be extreme, but not out of line with this moral regulation. The irony, therefore, of a situation where the most powerless member of the community is exalted to the status of goddess or an embodiment of honour of the community, should not be lost on anyone. In fact, if she were not powerless, she could not have been pushed into the mould of a symbol or disembodied into a metaphor. This metaphoric or symbolic exaltation is simultaneously an objectification of women and of "our" difference from "the West." Disembodiment and objectification are the foundation of violence against women, which cannot happen without a material or social base of domination. It is not an accident that the honour of this symbolic investiture is not conferred upon men, and that women have no choice about being chosen as symbolic or significatory objects.

The dehumanization involved in converting a person, an embodied socio-historical being, into a sign or symbol implies much more than an epistemological violence. It is based on the same principles that enabled a physical, social, and symbolic violence to be visited upon jews in pogroms and the holocaust, on various indigenous peoples in colonial genocides, and on Africans in slavery. Thus patriarchy, anti-Semitism, or racism, with or without fusing into each other, provide an overall social organization of relations of domination which extends from everyday-life repressions to extermination. The symbol is a formalization of actual violent, social relations which organize the society as a whole. It is a way of encoding, naming, and perpetuating them. This reality is evident in widow immolations in India, stoning of adulterous women in Pakistan, or female genital mutilation among some groups in Africa, to give a few examples. Discursivities entailed in these symbolic expressions mediate and stabilize violent social relations through various forms of textualization. They make room for elite males to be exonerated from responsibility as perpetrators of such social violence.

The significational figurations of women have been used as objects of hegemony by colonizers, nationalist elites and their analogues in Canada — the communities of non-white immigrants, and by the state. Women have become objects for creating history, but are given no role of their own to play in the making of it, except as victims of wars. The organization of societies in terms of gender has identified women with the private sphere, except at a symbolic level. This means an identification with "home," domesticity, and the family, which come into being through their activities and end up by being their enclosures.

The most prominent of the women signs in the contexts of nations and communities is that of the mother, the ultimate incarnation of the "good woman." The "goodness" of women in this extreme patriarchal incarnation, but in others as well, is manifested in a nurturing and sacrificing conduct at the service of the patriarchal family and equally patriarchal causes of larger collectivities, such as the nation or the community. Fear of disruption of this normative design comes chiefly from a fear of women's sexuality, which is, therefore, demonized and punished. The somewhat lesser disruptive source is the life of reason, which would put women in public spaces. Any move made by women in these directions is therefore considered to be "Western," "white," or "colonial," that is, treasonable to the greater "national" or community causes. But it is also "abnormal," as it would upset the sign of difference with which "our" co-opted male elite make political deals in multicultural terms or create attempts at cultural national resistance. It is important to note that both female sexuality and interest in rationality or education become threatening because they confer on women active roles which transgress the normative public-private divide. Containment and control of women through the normative mechanism of femininity underpin both proscriptions. In situations where such fully religious fundamentalist conduct cannot be enjoined, the proscriptive moral regulations still hold in a somewhat compromised or "modernized" manner. But it is not an exaggeration to say that the more women belonging to the community could be forced into its organizing religio-patriarchal norms and forms, the more the community could proclaim its definitively authentic status. Straying from these laid-down paths would call for censures of betrayal of a nature similar to those extended towards white women by white supremacist groups for betraying the empire, the "race," or the nation through miscegenation.

When we examine issues of patriarchal violence against women, it becomes apparent that the traditional community's social organization does not serve the greater good of the collectivity. Neither women nor less privileged men have their interests represented in it. The real benefit that it confers on males of all classes is great power over women and children, even men who are excluded or marginalized by the host society. This is not unlike national governments which cannot face up to international financial powers, but rule as dictators within national boundaries. In fact, the international or the multicultural national state's approval of them is dependent upon how well they can control these internal forces and their potential for opposition.

By a perverted extension of this logic the men of these communities are excused, even by anti-racist or otherwise feminist activists, for their generally sexist or even violent misconduct against women. Racism and class discrimination are held responsible for the rage that men vent on women, children, or homosexual members of their communities. This tolerance can extend up to severe abuse or even murder. Locking up women without their clothes, severe beating, mutilation or burning them with cigarette stubs, are some of the violences we have heard of. It is extraordinary how infrequently it is noted, if at all, that women too are subjects of colonialism and racism, and these oppressions are intensified by sexism or gross forms of patriarchy. It is a known fact that non-white women mostly work at worse paying and more menial jobs than their husbands, keep a double day of work inside and outside the home, and suffer from particularly humiliating forms of sexual harassment. In spite of all this, a woman does not often take out her frustration on her husband and children, as a man does. And certainly her mistreatment of them is never explained in the same terms, nor extenuated by the community and others for the same reasons, with which even the Canadian justice system credits abusive men. Whereas compromised and reduced masculinity of such men is noted sympathetically by scholars of colonialism and slavery, the compromised humanity of women, their punishment through hyper-femininity, rarely draws equal attention. If anything, a woman who wants to go beyond such roles and ascriptions, who is critical of patriarchy within the community, is often blamed for aiding and abetting in the colonial project of emasculation. Meanwhile, police and other forms of state and daily racist, social violence are directed against non-white women. The police murder of the sons of black women (and men) is as much a violence against their mothers (and fathers) as is the shooting of Sophia Cook or the strip search of Audrey Smith.[3]

V

I have outlined so far, and quite extensively, some salient aspects of the social problematic and certain specificities regarding violence against women in the community. Obviously a lot more remains to be said. But this is an attempt to break the silence I referred to at the beginning of my letter. I have tried to point towards a politics which, I hope, addresses the multiple social relations of power which organize our society. I have tried to show that a simplistic binary politics of self and other, of essentialist identities pitted against each other in a politics of cultural nationalism, is not a viable option for women. This reflection of cultural nationalism, of so-called multicultural community politics, does not erase racism or colonial oppression. In fact, the real struggle against the socially hegemonic forces and their expression in the Canadian state requires the perspective that I have offered. We cannot allow ourselves to be blackmailed in the name of cultural authenticity, identity, and community, any more than we can be duped by the mythologies of social democracy proffered by a racist and imperialist bourgeois state.

What awaits us is the political task of forging a real anti-racist feminism informed by a class analysis, with a critique of imperialism exposing the hoax of globalization. This politics cannot be brought to life if we stop only at a critique of patriarchal and gendered social organization. Such a critique, without an awareness and theorization of women as historical and social agents, would fall into the trap of showing women as victims of men and society. We must remember, then, that because women are also subjects of colonialism, racism, and class organization, because they also inhabit the same social relations as men, they too are part of the dynamics of resistance and domination. They have the same political needs, rights, and potentials as men — to be full citizens or members of nation states and to become agents in revolutionary politics.

It will not serve women to look for enclosed and co-opted identities in the name of family, god, nation, or the multicultural state — to live for their approbation. Our politics will have to be indifferent to special pleadings of arguments of spurious difference, but concentrate instead on the workings of the construction of difference through social relations of power, on the instruments of ruling. Developing a critical perception of sexist-racist social and cultural common sense and of the apparatus of the state, questioning laws that position "immigrants" in vulnerable roles within the political economy, questioning "multiculturalism" which co-opts and distorts popular political agency — these are our immediate tasks. Obviously they are not easy tasks, nor are results to be achieved instantly. Nor can they be carried on within the locked doors of community or identity politics. We, non-white women, women of "communities," must claim various political movements in Canada as our own. This means the women's movement and movements of resistance against state and class power, against pervasive and insidious racism and homophobia. Though it may sound like a tall order, it is possible to enter our politics through the door of particular "women's issues," for example, and come into the arena of a general political resistance. It is only in doing this that one can shape one's politics in ways that are nuanced by other struggles, where what comes out is the convergence of various politics against oppression, and not their separate directions. I don't think we need to fear a loss of specificity, of our selves, in a vast sea of abstractions or generalities controlled by others. If we can frame our critique and create organizations that challenge patriarchy, heterosexism, class, and "race" with even a semblance of integrity, we will create the bases for an embodied, social revolution. Needless to say, in this process we will have to redefine our friends and enemies, our notions of insiders and outsiders, and to whom, when, how, and about what we can talk. This open letter about our silence is only a very small experiment at that talk.

With love and solidarity,

Himani

NOTES

1   I am aware that calling people "non-white" is a debatable practice. I would not do so if I were to use it as a term denoting identity — namely, as a signification for *who we are*. I use this term as a political signifier, not an ontological one, to point out the hegemonic cause of our woes, namely racism. In this matter where we come from, our national cultures, are less significant than the fact that whoever is not "white" will fall within the purview of racialization and discrimination. For this purpose I prefer to use the expression "non-white," since the conventional terms "women of colour," "immigrants," etc. do not always do the job at hand.

2   Here we might, following Althusser, speak of being interpellated by the ideological apparatuses of the state, the state being understood as both an institution and a general political body. The political subjectivities and agencies of communities constructed through these processes are both conditional and subcontracted to current hegemonies.

3   See notes 20 and 21 in Chapter 2, "Geography Lessons."

Selected Additional Bibliography

SECTION I — BOOKS

This bibliographic section lists a selection of books pertaining to the multicultural debate.

Agnew, Vijay. *Resisting Discrimination: Women from Asia, Africa, and the Women's Movement in Canada.* Toronto: University of Toronto Press, 1996.

Alladin, Ibrahim. "Racism in Schools: Race, Ethnicity, and Schooling in Canada." Ed. Ibrahim Alladin. *Racism in Canadian Schools.* Toronto: Harcourt Brace, 1996.

Amit-Talai, Vered. "The Minority Circuit: Identity Politics and the Professionalization of Ethnic Activism." In *Resituating Identities,* ed. Vered Amit-Talai and Caroline Knowles, 89-114. Toronto: Broadview Press, 1996.

Andrew, Caroline. "Ethnicities, Citizenship and Feminisms: Theorizing the Political Practices of Intersectionality." In *Ethnicity and Citizenship: The Canadian Case,* ed. Jean Laponce and William Safran. London: Frank Cass, 1996.

Atwood, Margaret. *Survival: A Thematic Guide to Canadian Literature.* Toronto: Anansi, 1972.

Avery, Donald. *Reluctant Host: Canada's Response to Immigrant Workers.* Toronto: McClelland and Stewart, 1995.

Bakan, Abigail, and Daiva Stasiulis. *'Not One of the Family': Foreign Domestic Workers in Canada.* Toronto: University of Toronto Press, 1997.

Bannerji, Hamani, ed. *Returning the Gaze: Essays on Racism, Feminism and Politics.* Toronto: Sister Vision Press, 1993.

Bissoondath, Neil. *Selling Illusions: The Cult of Multiculturalism in Canada*. Toronto: Penguin Books, 1994.

Bolaria, B. Singh, and Peter S. Li. *Racial Oppression in Canada*. Toronto: Garamond Press, 1988.

Breton, Raymond, W. W. Isajiw, Warren E. Kalbach, and J. Reitz. *Ethnic Identity and Equality: Varieties of Experience in a Canadian City*. Toronto: University of Toronto Press, 1990.

Brodie, Janine. *Politics on the Margin*. Halifax: Fernwood Publishing, 1995.

Buchignani, N. L., D. M. Indra, and R. Srivastava. *Continuous Journey: A Social History of South Asians in Canada*. Toronto: McClelland and Stewart, 1985.

Burnet, Jean, and Howard Palmer. *Coming Canadians: An Introduction to a History of Canada's Peoples*. Toronto: McClelland and Stewart, 1988.

Cairns, H. Alan D. *Disruptions: Constitutional Struggles, from the Charter to Meech Lake*. Toronto: McClelland and Stewart, 1991.

Cardozo, Andrew, and Louis Musto, eds. *The Battle Over Multiculturalism*. Ottawa: Pearson-Shoyama Institute, 1997.

Carty, Linda, ed. *And Still We Rise: Feminist Political Mobilizing in Contemporary Canada*. Toronto: Women's Press, 1993.

Das Gupta, Tania. *Learning From Our History*. Toronto: Cross Cultural Communication Centre, 1986.

Draper, Paula, Franca Iacovetta, and Robert Ventresca, eds. *A Nation of Immigrants: Women, Workers and Communities in Canadian History, 1840s-1960s*. Toronto: University of Toronto Press, 1998.

Driedger, Leo, ed. *Ethnic Canada: Identities and Inequalities*. Toronto: Copp Clark Pitman Ltd., 1987.

Fine, Michelle, L. Weiss, L. C. Powell, and L. M. Wong, eds. *Off White: Readings on Race, Power and Society*. London: Routledge, 1997.

Fleras, Augie, and Jean Leonard Elliott. *Multiculturalism in Canada: The Challenge of Diversity*. Scarborough: Nelson Canada, 1992.

Frye, Northrop. *The Bush Garden: Essays on the Canadian Imagination*. Toronto: Anansi, 1971.

Gabriel, Christina. "One or the Other? 'Race,' Gender, and the Limits of Official Multiculturalism." In *Women and Canadian Public Policy*, ed. Janine Brodie, 173-95. Toronto: Harcourt Brace and Company, 1995.

Gannage, Charlene. *Double Day, Double Bind*. Toronto: Women's Press, 1986.

Glazer, Nathan. *We Are All Multiculturalists Now*. Cambridge: Harvard University Press, 1997.

Gutmann, Amy. *Multiculturalism and the 'Politics of Recognition.'* Princeton, NJ: Princeton University Press, 1992.

Hawkins, Freda. *Canada and Immigration: Public Policy and Public Concern*. Montreal and Kingston: McGill-Queen's University Press, 1988.

Henry, Frances, ed. *The Caribbean Diaspora in Toronto: Learning to Live With Racism*. Toronto: University of Toronto Press, 1994.

Henry, Frances, Carol Tator, Winston Mattis, and Tim Rees. *The Colour of Democracy: Racism in Canadian Society*. Toronto: Harcourt Brace, 1995.

Hryniuk, Stella, ed. *Twenty Years of Multiculturalism: Successes and Failures*. Winnipeg: St. John's College Press, 1992.

Hutcheon, Linda, and Marion Richmond, eds. *Other Solitudes: Canadian Multicultural Fictions*. Toronto: Oxford University Press, 1990.

Ignatieff, Michael. *Blood and Belonging: Journeys into the New Nationalism*. New York: Farrar, Straus & Giroux, 1993.

Israel, M., ed. *South Asian Diaspora in Canada: Six Essays*. Toronto: The Multicultural History Society of Ontario, 1987.

Jenson, Jane. "Citizenship Claims: Routes to Representation in a Federal System." In *Rethinking Federalism*, ed. Karen Knop et al., 99-118. Vancouver: University of British Columbia Press.

Kanungo, R. N., ed. *South Asians in Canadian Mosaic*. Montreal: The Kala Bharati Foundation, 1984.

Kukathas, Chandran, ed. *Multicultural Citizens: The Philosophy and Politics of Identity*. St. Leonards: Centre for Independent Studies, 1993.

Kurian, G., and R. Ghosh, eds. *Women in the Family and the Economy*. Westport, Connecticut: Greenwood Press, 1981.

Kymlica, Will. *Liberalism, Community and Culture*. Oxford: Clarendon Press, 1989.

———. *Multicultural Citizenship: A Liberal Theory of Minority Rights*. Oxford: Clarendon Press, 1995.

Li, Peter S. *The Chinese in Canada*. Toronto: Oxford University Press, 1988.

———. *Ethnic Inequality in a Class Society*. Toronto: Wall and Thompson Press, 1988.

———, ed. *Race and Ethnic Relations in Canada*. Toronto: Oxford University Press, 1990.

Li, Peter S., and B. Singh Bolaria, eds. *Racial Minorities in Multicultural Canada*. Toronto: Garamond Press, 1983.

Mackey, Eva. *The House of Difference: Cultural Politics and National Identity in Canada*. London: Routledge, 1999.

Manning, Preston. *The New Canada*. Toronto: Macmillan, 1992.

Ng, Roxanna. *The Politics of Community Services: Immigrant Women, Class and the State*. Toronto: Garamond Press, 1988.

Nourbese Philip, Marlene. *Frontiers: Selected Essays and Writings on Racism and Culture, 1984-1992*. Stratford, Ontario: Mercury Press, 1992.

Pal, Leslie A. *Interests of State: The Politics of Language, Multiculturalism, and Feminism in Canada*. Montreal and Kingston: McGill-Queen's University Press, 1993.

———. *Immigration and Ethnic Conflict*. Toronto: Macmillan, 1988.

Samuda, R. J., J. W. Berry, and M. LaFerriere, eds. *Multiculturalism in Canada: Social and Educational Perspectives*. Toronto: Allyn and Bacon Inc., 1984.

Satchevich, Vic, ed. *Racism and the Incorporation of Foreign Labour*. London: Routledge, 1991.

———. *Deconstruction a Nation: Immigration, Multiculturalism and Racism in '90s Canada*. Halifax: Fernwood Publishing, 1992.

———. *Multi-Ethnic Canada: Identities and Inequalities*. Toronto: Oxford University Press, 1996.

Smith, E. Y. *Canadian Multiculturalism: The Solution or the Problem*. New York: Pergamon Press, 1983.

Thornhill, Esmerelda. "Focus on Black Women!" In *Race, Class, Gender: Bonds and Barriers*, ed. J. Vorst et al., 27-38. Toronto: Garamond Press and Society for Socialist Studies, 1991.

Webber, Jeremy. *Reimagining Canada: Language, Culture, Community, and the Canadian Constitution*. Montreal and Kingston: McGill-Queen's University Press, 1994.

Whitaker, Reg. *Double Standard: The Secret History of Canadian Immigration*. Toronto: Lester & Orpen Dennys, 1987.

———. *Canadian Immigration Policy Since Confederation*. Saint John, NB: Canadian Historical Association, 1991.

SECTION II – GOVERNMENT DOCUMENTS

Prior to its use by the Royal Commission on Bilingualism and Biculturalism, the term "multicultural" or "multiculturalism" did not figure prominently in governmental or constitutional documents. Although the B and B Commission did not define the meaning of "multicultural" or "multiculturalism," it was the first, amongst many governmental documents to follow, that sought to describe and frame a governmental understanding of Canadian culture and heritage as inherently "multicultural." The citations in this bibliographic section are comprised of key Canadian governmental documents that were commissioned to frame and legitimate this state of *multi*-culture.

Abella, R. S. *Report of the Commission on Equality in Employment.* Ottawa: Ministry of Supply and Services Canada, 1984.

Berry, John W., Rudolf Kalin, and Donald M. Taylor. *Multiculturalism and Ethnic Attitudes in Canada.* Ottawa: Supply and Services Canada, 1977.

Beaudoin, Gerald, and Dorothy Dobbie. *Report of the Special Joint Committee on a Renewed Canada,* 28 February 1992. Ottawa: Supply and Services Canada, 1992.

Billingsley, Brenda, and Leon Muczynski. *No Discrimination Here?: Toronto Employers and the Multi-Racial Workforce.* Toronto: Social Planning Council of Metropolitan Toronto, 1985.

Canada. The Constitution Act (Including the Canadian Charter of Rights and Freedoms). Ottawa: Supply and Services Canada, 1982.

Canada. *Shaping Canada's Future Together: Proposal.* Ottawa: Supply and Services Canada, 1991.

Canada. Canadian Multiculturalism Act. *Chapter 24, An Act for the Preservation and Enhancement of Multiculturalism in Canada.* Ottawa: Queen's Printer, 1988.

Canada. Canadian Multiculturalism Act. *Chapter 27 An Act for the Preservation and Enforcement of Multiculturalism in Canada.* Ottawa: Queen's Printer, 1988.

Canada. Corporate Policy Branch of the Department of Canadian Heritage. "Canadian Multiculturalism Act Briefing Book: Clause by Clause Analysis." Unpublished document released under the Access to Information Act.

Canada. Corporate Review Branch of the Department of Canadian Heritage. *Strategic Evaluation of Multiculturalism Programs: Final Report.* Ottawa: Corporate Review Branch of the Department of Canadian Heritage, 1996.

Canada. Department of Justice. *Preserving Identity by Having Many Identities: A Report on Multiculturalism.* Ottawa: Department of Justice, 1991.

Canada. House of Commons. *Multiculturalism: Building the Canadian Mosaic. Report of the Standing Committee on Multiculturalism.* Ottawa: Supply and Services Canada, 1987.

Canada. Multiculturalism and Citizenship Corporate Policy Branch. "Multiculturalism Policy Strategy Document: A Proposal." Unpublished document released under the Access to Information Act, 1987.

Canada. Multiculturalism and Citizenship Canada. *Resource Guide: Eliminating Racial Discrimination.* Ottawa: Queen's Printer, 1990.

Canada. Royal Commission on Bilingualism and Biculturalism. *Report of the Royal Commission on Bilingualism and Biculturalism, Vol. IV: The Cultural Contribution of the Other Ethnic Groups.* Ottawa: Queen's Printer, 1969.

Estable, A. *Immigrant Women in Canada — Current Issues*. Ottawa: Canadian Advisory Council on the Status of Women, March 1986.

Spicer, Keith. *Citizen's Forum on Canada's Future: Report to the People and Government of Canada*. Ottawa: Supply and Services Canada, 1991.

SECTION III — ACADEMIC JOURNALS

This bibliographic section lists a selection of articles from various academic journals pertaining to the multicultural debate.

Abu-Laban, Yasmeen, and Daiva Stasiulis. "Ethnic Pluralism under Siege: Popular and Partisan Opposition to Multiculturalism." *Canadian Public Policy* 18, no. 4 (December 1992): 365-86.

Agnew, V. "Educated Indian Women in Ontario." *Polyphony: Women and Ethnicity* 8, no. 1-2 (1986): 70-72.

Angel, Sumayya. "The Multiculturalism Act of 1988." *Multiculturalism* 11, no. 3 (1988): 25-7.

Aponiuk, Natalia. "Ethnic Literature, Minority Writing, Literature in Other Languages, Hyphenated-Canadian Literature: Will It Ever Be Canadian?" *Canadian Ethnic Studies* 23, no. 1 (1996): 1-7.

Bakan, Abigail and Daiva Stasiulis. "Foreign Domestic Worker Policy in Canada and the Social Boundaries of Citizenship." *Science and Society* 58, no. 1 (1994): 1-33.

————. "Making the Match: Domestic Placement Agencies and the Racialization of Women's Household Work." *Signs* 29, no. 2 (1995): 303-35.

Bennett, Donna. "English Canada's Postcolonial Complexities." *Essays on Canadian Writing* 51, no. 2 (Winter 1993/Spring 1994): 164-210.

Buchignani, N. L. "South Asian Canadians and the Ethnic Mosaic." *Canadian Ethnic Studies* 11, no. 1 (1979): 48-67.

Burnet, Jean. "Multiculturalism, Immigration and Racism." *Canadian Ethnic Studies* 7, no. 1 (1979): 35-9.

Cassim, M. "East Indian Women Farm Workers." *Multiculturalism* 11, no. 4 (1979): 14-15.

Creese, Gillian. "Immigration Policies and the Creation of an Ethnically Segmented Working Class." *Alternate Routes* 7 (1984): 1-34.

Creese, Gillian, and Daiva Stasiulis. "Introduction: Intersections of Gender, Race, Class and Sexuality." *Studies in Political Economy* 51 (Fall 1996): 5-14.

Das Gupta, Tania. "South Asian Women at Work." *Ethnocultural Notes and Events* (February/March 1981).

———. "Looking under the Mosaic: South Asian Immigrant Women." *Polyphony: Women and Ethnicity* 8, no. 1-2 (1986): 67-69.

Davetian, Benet. "Out of the Melting Pot and into the Fire: An Essay on Neil Bissoondath's Book on Multiculturalism." *Canadian Ethnic Studies* 26, no. 3 (1994): 135-140.

Davey, Frank. "Cultural Mischief: A Practical Guide to Multiculturalism." *Canadian Literature* 155 (Winter 1997): 194-7.

Duclos, Nitya. "Disappearing Women: Racial Minority Women in Human Rights Cases." *Canadian Journal of Women and the Law* 6, no. 1 (1993): 25-51.

Fawcett, Brian. "Some Questions and Issues about the New Nationalism." *Journal of Canadian Studies* 31, no. 3 (1996): 189-192.

Giles, Wenona, and Valerie Preston. "The Domestication of Women's Work: A Comparison of Chinese and Portuguese Women Workers." *Studies in Political Economy* 51 (Fall 1996): 147-82.

Godard, Barbara. "The Discourse of the Other: Canadian Literature and the Question of Ethnicity." *The Massachusetts Review* 31, no. 1-2 (Spring-Summer 1990): 153-184.

Gunew, Sneja. "Multicultural Multiplicities: Canada, U.S.A., Australia." *Meanjin* 52, no. 3 (Spring 1993): 447-89.

Gutmann, Amy. "The Challenge of Multiculturalism to Political Ethics." *Philosophy and Public Affairs* 22, no. 3 (1993): 171-206.

Hage, Ghassan. "Locating Multiculturalism's Other: A Critique of Practical Tolerance." *New Formations* 24 (1994): 19-34.

———. "White Nation: Fantasies of White Supremacy in a Multicultural Society." *New Internationalist* 311 (April 1999): 32.

Harles, John. "Multiculturalism, National Identity, and National Integration: The Canadian Case." *International Journal of Canadian Studies* 17 (Spring 1998): 215-45.

Iyer, Nitya. "Categorical Denials: Equality Rights and the Shaping of Social Identity." *Queen's Law Journal* 19, no. 1 (Fall 1993): 179-207.

Jenson, Jane. "Naming Nations: Making Nationalist Claims in Canadian Public Discourse." *Canadian Review of Sociology and Anthropology* 30, no. 3 (1993): 337-58.

Kadar, Marlene. "Discourse of Ordinariness and 'Multicultural History.'" *Essays on Canadian Writing* 60 (Winter 1996): 119-38.

Kay, Jonathan. "Explaining the Modern Backlash against Multiculturalism." *Policy Options politiques* 19, no. 4 (May 1998): 30-4.

Kotash, Myrna. "Ethnic Adventures of the Third Generation." *Journal of Canadian Studies* 30, no. 2 (Summer 1995): 124-9.

Kulchyski, Peter. "Aboriginal Peoples and Hegemony in Canada." *Journal of Canadian Studies* 30, no. 1 (Spring 1995): 60-68.

————. "Bush Culture for a Bush Country: An Unfinished Manifesto." *Journal of Canadian Studies* 31, no. 3 (1996): 192-196.

Li, Xiaoping. "Response to Neil Bissoondath's (Selling) Illusions." *Journal of Canadian Studies* 30, no. 2 (Summer 1995): 130-7.

Mackey, Eva. "Postmodernism and Cultural Politics in a Multicultural Nation: Contests over Truth in the 'Into the Heart of Africa' Controversy." *Public Culture* 7, no. 2 (Winter 1995): 430-1.

Moodley, Kogila. "Canadian Multiculturalism as Ideology." *Ethnic and Racial Studies* 6, no. 3 (1983): 320-31.

Padolsky, Enoch. "Ethnicity and Race: Canadian Minority Writing at a Crossroads." *Journal of Canadian Studies* 31, no. 3 (1996): 129-147.

Pal, Leslie A. "Interests of State: The Politics of Language, Multiculturalism and Feminism in Canada." *Labour/Le travail* 35 (Spring 1995): 389-92. And also in *Journal of Canadian Studies* 30, no. 3 (Fall 1995): 223-31. And also in *Canadian Journal of Political Science* 31, no. 1 (March 1997): 149-50.

Pickles, Katie. "Forgotten Colonizers: The Imperial Order Daughters of the Empire (IODE) and the Canadian North." *Canadian Geographer* 42, no. 2 (Summer 1998): 193-204.

Raviot, Jean-Robert. "Plural Cultures, Contested Territories: A Critique of [Will] Kymlicka." *Canadian Journal of Political Science* 30, no. 2 (June 1997): 211-34.

Ravitch, Diane. "Multiculturalism: E Pluribus Plures." *The American Scholar* 59, no. 3 (1990): 337-54.

Razach, Sherene. "What Is to Be Gained by Looking White People in the Eye? Culture, Race and Gender in Cases of Sexual Violence." *Signs* 19, no. 4 (1994): 894-923.

Russell, Claudette. "When the Melting Pot Boils Over: If Immigrants Come to Canada Intent on Preserving All Their Culture, Then Why Are They Really Coming?" *Policy Options politiques* 12, no. 9 (November 1991): 20-1.

Tully, James. "Strange Multiplicity: Constitutionalism in an Age of Diversity." *Canadian Review of Sociology and Anthropology* 34, no. 2 (May 1997): 238-9.

Ungerleider, Charles S. "Immigration, Multiculturalism, and Citizenship: The Development of the Canadian Social Justice Infrastructure." *Canadian Ethnic Studies* 24, no. 3 (1992): 7-22.

Verduyn, Christl. "Disjunctions: Place, Identity and Nation in 'Minority' Literatures in Canada." *Canadian Issues* 20 (1998): 164-175.

ABOUT THE COVER

The design on the cover is a traditional North American quilt pattern known as log cabin, made of 100% cotton fabric, designed and printed in India, and quilted in India at the Schroff Self Help Centre.

The Schroff Self Help Centre was founded in 1972 to provide income and training to families of estate workers and those in the surrounding community, and currently employs eighty artisans making clothing and textiles. The centre provides recreational facilities for the artisans' children, day care, and an educational allowance to enable workers' children to attend school.

The Schroff Self Help Centre is one of many small producers doing business with Bridgehead, a company that links Canadians with small producers in the developing world through fair trade. Bridgehead promotes social, economic and environmental justice by purchasing directly from small producers, minimizing intermediaries; paying fair prices set by producers, based on the real costs of labour and production; facilitating access to credit for small producers; providing technical assistance to producers to improve products and processes; encouraging concern for employees, and employee participation in the running of businesses; and supporting and encouraging sustainable environmental practices.